THE ADOBE BOOK

The Adobe Book

by JOHN F. O'CONNOR

Illustrations and photographs

by the author.

Ancient City Press

P.O. Box 5401   Santa Fe, New Mexico 87502

Cover photograph: Hyatt Studio-Gallery
in Casa Viejas, Upper Canyon Road,
Santa Fe, New Mexico

Cover photograph by Peter Weiss
Cover design by Mary Powell

Fourth Printing

ISBN 0-941270-19-X

Printed in the United States of America

Contents

Foreword

Since you are reading this book, you must already have some interest in building or owning an Adobe Home, so read on, we'll try to whet that interest and ensnare you in our adobe web.

All of the usual benefits of home-ownership accrue to the builder of an adobe home, plus several rather unique assets. Perhaps the first benefit should be labeled aesthetics, as no other style fits as well into the great American Southwest terrain as does adobe. The soft lines, natural colors and adaptability of this earthen material blend into the landscape, do not intrude, but enhance the environment. A secondary asset is that of superior insulating quality, so that the adobe home is easy to heat in the winter, yet remains cool in the heat of the summer. This insulating quality is attained only with traditional adobe construction, meaning walls a minimum of two feet thick. This massive construction has a beauty of its own, so that the home appears blended into the site, rather than stuck upon it.

Among the other assets of adobe are longevity and economics. An adobe home will outlast almost any alternate construction material, given even the most minimal maintenance. The economics of adobe should be self-evident, but have often been deliberately obscured by the purveyors of competing materials. The cost of an adobe home completely built by a contractor may exceed that of frame or cinder-block, but if you are going to compare your adobe home to a developer's tract housing, forget about this book, you don't want it.

For the man who rolls his own, an adobe home may be built by him for a lower total dollar expenditure than any other type, simply because there are less components to purchase. The biggest part of total cost in an adobe home is labor, and brother, there sure is God's plenty of that. You may make your own adobe blocks or purchase them, depending upon your own balance of time and money. If funds are very short, make the adobes with your own hands. If time is the critical element, you may have to order the adobes ready-made.

Aside from the lower dollar cost when built by your own hands, the other aspect of economics of adobe is market value of the finished home. Depending upon the time and locale, a well-built adobe home will bring a substantially higher price on sale than will a house of wood-frame, brick or block with the exact same area and facilities. As the old bromide says, "you gets what you pays for."

We hope that you do decide to build your own adobe home, and so offer this book to provide some guidance and assistance in that effort. In a subject with as many inherent variables as housing, it will be neither practical nor very smart to set forth a group of definite, rigid requirements. Therefore, throughout this work, we will attempt to lead you through the maze of problems, point out alternative solutions, offer suggestions, and hopefully provide enough data for you to surmount the problem and make the decision for yourself.

The construction of your own adobe home may well be one of the most self-gratifying major undertakings of your life. It is a truly big job, and must be approached with a full realization of the enormous amount of time and labor that it will require. This is not a project to while away a few idle hours, or to satisfy a passing whim, as its completion may consume all of your spare time for several years. The planning alone will take many of your hours, and must be well and truly done. Consider the time spent on planning as a part of the investment in your home, as each hour so spent may save frustration, and countless hours of construction labor. Before you turn a single spadeful of earth, the complete project should be planned down to the last ultimate details. If you do not, you will certainly find yourself wrecking out and removing hard-won portions of the house, solely because you forgot something, and have to tear out finished work to make room for the overlooked need.

Where are you going to build this house? Many people have spent months, or even years, designing and planning their adobe home, then bought a piece of land to build upon, only to find that the physical conditions of the purchased site required extensive revisions to the dream house design. We feel that a home must be designed to fit a specific site, rather than attempting to warp the site to accommodate a preconceived home design. An economic consideration here, you might select and purchase a site, then complete your planning and final design while you pay off the land cost. Many financial institutions will make a construction loan, when a paid-off land site is offered as security.

There are many general decisions to be made before arriving at this point, the major one being whether or not you can really do it. This sounds like a very simple question, but it really isn't. Carefully consider whether the wonderful satisfaction of building your own adobe home from the ground up is worth to you the big effort that must be made. Also, and very important, is the basic question of whether you are physically capable of performing all the hard labor and the varied types of skilled work to be done in the building of the home. This is another area where planning pays off, as you should become aware of needs and capabilities in time to avoid serious complications. In evaluating your own talents and strengths, you will discover the areas in which you need help, even to the point of contracting certain portions of the work.

Preliminary planning will resolve many general questions before you can get down to actual detailed design. You will find yourself making list after list of items considered for the home, changing and refining until you at long last decide how things are to be. Think of all the homes you've admired, the things you liked or disliked in each, and all that you need and want in this, your own adobe home. The multitude of necessary decisions at this stage is staggering and bewildering. How big or small must the home be? How many, and what size and shape rooms? What type of heating plant? Which type of lighting and wiring? How many different codes do we have to conform to? Where should the home be built? Pueblo or Territorial, or, god forbid, modern? What kind and how many of the appliances should be built-in? Almost certainly one or more fireplaces, but where and what size? How much will it cost, and how will it be financed? These, and other questions, will arise before pencil kisses paper to start detailed design. Which even creates another question, do you design the home yourself, or retain an engineer or architect to do it for you? These decisions are all to be yours, no one else can make them for you.

Before you get too deep into your detailed planning, you must check with the various government regulatory agencies that you have to contend with; that is, the city, county or state building, electrical, plumbing, zoning, or other boards or inspectors. There are a multitude of these authorities around the country, and their jurisdictions often overlap, and even wind up with conflicting regulations. Of course, before buying any property, the zoning has to be investigated, simply to discover whether or not you can build your adobe home on that site.

Investigate all aspects of construction codes where you wish to build, as requirements may change drastically within separate jurisdictions. For instance, some plumbing codes permit the use of P.V.C. plastic soil lines, but not interior lines, while other areas may demand cast iron piping throughout. These and other variations demand that you find out what you must do, before you can readily determine what you want to do. Therefore, in all aspects of your adobe home, plan and check each proposed problem solution, so as to ascertain whether the method is legal, practical, economical and aesthetic. As we keep insisting, plan, plan, and yet again, plan.

This book will attempt to assist you in the evaluation of many problems, but will not make the decisions for you. Insofar as possible in a limited work, alternate methods, means and styles will be set forth, so choose your own poison. In the last analysis, it's all completely up to you, so have at it.

In today's money-mad world, the first item to become obsolete is a cost estimate. Therefore, we will make no serious attempt to evaluate the various costs encountered in the completion of your adobe home. The cost factors of labor, land, materials and equipment are inherently variable in time, location, quantities, quality and scope. The same labor that might cost $5.00 per man-hour in Dallas could possibly be obtained for $1.75 in Lower Colonias. Land cost is an extreme variable, depending upon size, location, time, demand and accessibility. A valid, accurate cost estimate may be derived for a specific house design, with certain features and equipment, to be constructed at a definite time and place. However, it is an exercise in futility to even attempt to approximate cost factors in a book whose scope is the whole spectrum of adobe homes. So, being not quite completely stupid, we won't even try.

But total dollar cost will be perhaps the major factor in the planning of your adobe home project. During preliminary planning, you must make many decisions affecting the total expenditure for your home. The choices in materials, trim, heating plant, lighting systems and all other factors will be influenced by cost over or under somewhat comparable items. A prime method to make these choices is through comparison shopping, as most of the suppliers or dealers in such goods will give excellent cooperation through providing cost quotations and advice. In this respect, the dealer who does not want to be bothered in giving the time for this aid may be a poor choice for a materials source. Don't overestimate your own abilities, and don't be afraid to ask questions. If you learned something from the answer, it wasn't a dumb question.

Don't select major items for your home on the basis of initial purchase cost alone. If you do, they could become the most expensive dollars you ever saved. Remember that he who considers price only, is the legitimate prey of the sharpie and fast-buck artist. While original purchase price is important, the really significant factor is the total-life cost of an item. The total-life cost is the purchase price, plus installation, operating and maintenance costs, spread over the length of useful service life. It doesn't make too much sense to save thirty or forty dollars on purchase price for an item that lasts only half as long, and costs twice as much in fuel or operating cost, as an item slightly more expensive at initial cost. So again and again, ask questions, questions, and still more questions. Always check into service cost and availability, efficiency, operating cost and useful service life of the item, whether it be a simple switch, a pump or a complete heating plant.

Labor cost will be significant in your adobe home, whether your own time or that of specialty contractors. Your own time and labor do have definite dollar value, so be realistic during your planning and evaluate your own capabilities. The time to hire an expert is before the item of work has started, not after you have fouled it up beyond repair. Remember that it is no reflection upon you that you can't perform certain tasks or don't know specific skills, as no one can do everything. So be smart, select the work you either can't or don't wish to do, then hire an expert to do it for you. It may cost more in dollars, but it will be well worth it in savings in time, worry, frustration, and even possible injuries.

A word here on contracting; it is always wise to have the work covered by a written contract, or even a simple letter of intent. A written contract or work order should set forth exactly what you want done, and how much you are going to pay for it. For instance, don't just call up "good old Joe" and tell him to come out and do your wiring. Even if he's a friend, you could wind up with a finished or incomplete job that you didn't want or need, at a cost that you hadn't intended to pay. Investigate, ask questions, make the decision, and then get it in writing. It can save lost time and money, useless arguments, and produce the end result desired.

Complete as much of the general planning as possible before you go down to details, to help make all of the major decisions early enough to avoid excessive revisions in the detail plans. We can't emphasize too much the value of time spent in general planning, as the big decisions will aid in forcing the little decisions into place. Be firm and realistic while assessing your home-size demands, as it may be more practicable to add room later to the existing home, than to try to cut back on size and money while the house is under construction. You will presumably be doing this project in your spare time, so don't try too hard to hold yourself to a rigid time schedule. One of the variations of Parkinson's Law might read, "Everything takes longer to do than the time span within which you planned to do it." Relax, don't get too uptight over the inevitable delays and frustrations, as you will actually do better work if you are not harassing yourself by trying to push too hard. Enjoy your work, it's just not worth it all if you don't.

Building your own adobe home will bring with it abundant personal gratification. Watching your progress as the walls rise, the home gradually growing toward completion, offers a great pride in the fruits of your sweat and aching back. For there is no gainsaying that it will be seemingly endless, dirty, hard, wrenching manual labor. Almost every day throughout the hopefully many years you live in this home, you can look around and remember the little problem here, the item that went smooth as silk there, the big frustrating delay there, and sit back and enjoy.

To some folks, life in a home that you helped to build with your own hands may be the consummation of a large portion of life's aspirations. You probably intend to live in this home for most of your remaining years, so don't skimp on too many things. Attempt to provide all of the amenities you desire, as over the years, like everyone else, you may regret the niceties you omitted from the home because of cost or lack of planning. Which brings us around again to the bit continually urged herein, there simply is no substitute for good planning.

Go through all of this book, read and study the alternate offerings set forth, then plan, plan, and yet again, plan. Don't hold yourself down too much, try to be as realistic about the multitude of decisions as you can be, get expert help when you need it, and then go to it, and good luck!

CHAPTER I

Adobe History

Adobe is among the most ancient of all of History's building materials, and one of the most unsung. Although associated with only the Great Indian - Hispano - American Southwest in the minds of most, adobe has been used in home-building since long before the dawn of recorded history.

Archaeologists, architects, historians and others have written extensively of the massive stone fortresses of Vauban, the glories of Roman roads, bridges and aqueducts, the stone ruins of Greece and other antiquities, but few have concerned themselves with the adobe-type homes of the ordinary people throughout the ages. The fabled Hanging Gardens of Babylon, once one of the wonders of a bygone world, were undoubtedly built primarily of a form of adobe-mud-brick construction. Throughout the arid regions of this earth, from the ruins of storied Tyre and Nineveh to the still-inhabited Pueblos of Taos and Acoma, surviving examples of adobe construction abound, with buildings from these highly different areas exhibiting construction details of great similarity. It would seem that, no matter what the problem of any day or folk, men of all races, times and places have independently arrived at almost identical solutions.

Large segments of the ancient cities of the Middle East, Hebraic and Arabic, were of adobe construction, in part due to the scarcity and high cost of other materials, but also influenced by the insulating qualities of thick adobe walls. Great lords and mighty kings imported materials and skilled labor to raise lofty stone edifices to reflect their own glory, but the people built their homes with sun-dried adobe mud bricks. It may be amusing to realize that various authorities now state that many adobe ruins predate the Great Pyramid of Ghiza.

Adobe has always been a material of the people. Its use has generally been confined to the arid regions of the earth, due to the unique adaptability of adobe to such locales, the cost or scarcity of other materials, and the comparative ease of adobe construction. No single geographic locale nor any ethnic group or race may claim credit for the origin of adobe-type construction, since examples of this type of home-building have been found, and are still being built, in all of the semi-arid regions of the world. The parallel use and uncoordinated development of adobe on an almost world-wide basis is thus but another testimony to the resources and intelligence of all mankind.

Among the many virtues of adobe is its comparative simplicity of construction, which permits the use of unskilled labor, and is thus particularly suited to the needs of the Southwestern do-it-yourself homebuilder. Except for the adobe material itself, the ancient adobe home or pueblo bears little resemblance to the modern adobe hacienda, of both of which so many spectacular examples are to be found in the Santa Fe area. The ancient adobe, like all individual homes of those times, was little more than four tiny walls and a roof, often with hide-covered openings for doors and windows. The modern adobe home can be anything that the imagination and purse of the owner may produce, from a simple one-bedroom home to a magnificent, rambling Casa.

The very origin of the term "adobe" is somewhat vague and ill-defined, and subject to much argument among so-called authorities. Many sources insist it derives from the Spanish word "adobar," meaning "to knead," others state it comes from Spanish and Moroccan roots meaning "to mix" or "to puddle," while still others say that adobe originated with the Arab word "atob," meaning "sun-dried brick." As all of the etymological authorities do not agree on the derivation of the word "adobe," it is pointless to further belabor an obscure and age-old origin, as we are concerned with the use of adobe, not the source of the word. The usage of the term is itself very loose, as adobe may refer to the bricks made, to the soil used to make the bricks, or to the final product, the home.

On the North American continent, the use of adobe in several fashions was prevalent in the Southwest long before the arrival of the Conquistadores. The ruins of these varying adobe-type structures still survive in the Rio Grande

Valley, the Gila and the Salt River valleys and in what are now the Navajo, Ute, Apache, Hopi, and Pueblo areas of northern Arizona and New Mexico and the southern portions of Utah and Colorado. These ruins cover the entire spectrum of adobe construction, ranging from simple mud-daubed jacals, adobe-mortared stone, or solid rammed-earth walls, to complete Pueblo complexes built from adobe bricks. The early native adobe bricks were molded by hand, not set and packed in wooden forms. These primitive bricks varied considerably in shape and size, obviously resulting differences in applications, strengths or whims of the users. Shapes and sizes ranged from round balls rammed into layers, through tapered bricks laid in courses, loose mud placed and rammed into monoliths, to adobe bricks laid, faced and mortared almost identically to those still in use today.

Even now, little agreement may be obtained among the many sources and authorities on the optimum size for adobe bricks. Indeed, there are almost as many brick sizes as there are sources. This variation lends individuality and charm to the adobe home, as the builder may choose the size that suits his needs best. If the adobe bricks are to be purchased, you are limited to the size produced by the local sources, but those who make their own may set the brick size as they wish, and should be based upon the wall-thickness desired and the physical strength of the builders.

The arrival of the Conquistadores in the Southwest therefore only accelerated and refined the local use of adobe in home-building. The Pueblos in particular had brought the art of adobe to a high level of refinement, the structures being quite similar to those known by the Spaniards. What is now known as the "Pueblo" style adobe home resulted from the blend of Spanish and Indian influences. This style, with its soft contours, natural round vigas, and simple facade, can be utilized for a beautiful, comfortable home which will fit well into the landscape.

The arrival of the Americans in greater numbers into the Southwest resulted in the creation of the style now called "Territorial," which is a blend of Spanish, American Colonial, Arabic and other influences. The basic structure is usually identical to the Pueblo, but is more elaborate, with tile or fired brick copings, squared vigas and columns, formal trim in shutters, frames and doors, in general a more rigid, detailed facade. As always, the choice between these basic styles for your adobe home becomes strictly a matter of personal preference.

CHAPTER II

Adobe Soil

The one basic material required for all adobe homes is dirt. Perhaps you prefer the use of other terms, such as adobe soil, earthen material, or different usages, but they all come down to the basic source, which is dirt. Before you can start with your adobe home, you must first determine whether the proper variety of dirt is available in your immediate vicinity. So, this chapter will discuss the various properties of adobe-type soils to aid you in the investigation and solution of your basic materials problems. Insofar as possible, we will attempt to avoid extremely technical language and procedures, and in so doing, we may arouse the ire of our peers in the engineering and architecture professions, but this book is for you, not for them.

There are several basic methods for construction of adobe homes, from laying adobe blocks like brick-work, rammed-earth walls to wattle and daub. We feel that the adobe block method is vastly preferable for a multitude of reasons, not the least of which is that this method is the entire premise of this book. At this point, we will set out a brief discussion of these alternate methods for your edification, then return to the adobe block.

The rammed earth method has been highly advocated by some authorities, and does have some definite advantages, but also has considerable drawbacks. In this method, walls are formed in a continuous monolith by ramming moist soil into place inside heavy form-work. Generally, a section of wall is completed, the forms are removed and moved over or up, and the ramming process is continued until all walls have been finished. A well made rammed-earth wall is extremely durable, and may last for centuries. However, the complexity of the formwork and the skilled labor required for this method generally rule it out for the do-it-yourself home-builder. It is not a method that lends itself well to part-time construction. The form-work is quite heavy, and must be very well made and quite precisely set up to control the dimensions and strength of the wall section. The adobe soil and moisture content must be closely controlled to prevent cracking of the wall during the drying process, and the ramming itself is a lot of work that must be well done to produce uniform results. Also, a team of semi-skilled men is required to set the heavy forms, tie them down, and ram the earth into the forms. To us, the disadvantages of higher labor cost, danger of cracking, and the need for closer technical control greatly outweigh whatever advantages the rammed-earth method may offer.

The wattle and daub method is primitive and obsolete. In this method, a framework of posts and poles is built, then branches and reeds are woven among the poles. A mud plaster is then forced into and over this network to complete the wall. This method is highly susceptible to cracking, and even falling apart, and demands almost constant maintenance. Even when well done, this method in no way results in an adequate product for modern use.

So, we return to our preference, and we hope yours, adobe blocks. This method is by far the simplest, and can produce results equal to, or better than, any other technique offered for adobe construction. It is one of the most popular adobe methods, and is perhaps one of the most ancient of home construction modes.

With proper planning and a lot of hard work, almost anyone can build a home with adobe block. The basic elements of this method sound quite simple, but of course are not. First, the adobe soil must be found and dug out of the ground. Then, the soil is mixed with water, and whatever stabilizer is decided upon, and placed into forms to dry and cure. After the blocks have cured, and the foundation of the home has been completed, one places the adobe blocks in layers or "courses" to build the wall. The adobe blocks are held together with a mortar of the same material mixture as the blocks themselves. When all of this has been done, one simply places the beams or "vigas" across the walls, erects ceiling and roof, and then moves into the house.

Now that certainly sounds simple, doesn't it? We all know that it isn't quite that easy, or you wouldn't be reading this book. But we shall attempt to lead you down the garden path to the data you will need to make all the decisions for your adobe home. One of the great advantages of the adobe block method is its basic simplicity, and its ready adaptability to your own needs, in respect to cost, time, space and skill. After you have planned your house and selected the site, or even before, your first major construction need will be the adobe blocks themselves. Some of you would have said that the foundation comes first, but you are not quite correct. The foundation must be designed to support what is placed upon it, so the adobe wall thickness and height is first determined, and this in turn is subject to the dimensions of the adobe blocks used.

You must then decide whether to purchase the adobe blocks, or to make them yourself. In cash outlay, it is cheapest to make them yourself if there is a deposit of suitable adobe soil on or near your site. In terms of the value or scarcity of your time, it may be more economic to purchase the blocks. In this case, you are limited to the sizes of adobe blocks on the local market. If you make your own, you may make the blocks in any proportional size that is most convenient. That is, the size whose multiples will produce the wall thickness you desire, and that still is of an individual weight that you can handle without undesirable strain.

At long last, after all of this discussion, we come back to the basic purpose of this chapter, what kind of dirt or soil you use to manufacture your adobe blocks. In order to properly answer this question, we have to make a short dissertation on soils and their various properties.

It should become obvious that not all soils are suitable for making adobe blocks, so we will set forth some of the broad guidelines and discuss them for you. In general, there are five major varieties of soils; i.e., gravels, sands, silts, clays, and organic soils. To further complicate matters, these soils may not often be found in a "pure" state for each variety, but are often intermixed with rocks or another variety. The variable properties of these soil types are set out in the following paragraphs.

GRAVEL is made up of fairly coarse pieces of rock ranging from ¼″ to 3″ in their largest dimension. For the purpose of this book, any rock over 3″ in size is a stone or boulder, not gravel. The individual pieces of rock in gravel may be any shape, round, flat, angular, with either rough or smooth edges, and may include almost any rock from granite to limestone, or any other type.

Gravel may be found in the beds of swift streams, dry beds, glacial areas and around mountains. If the material in question breaks up or gets soft after being soaked in water for a day or more, it is not gravel. Gravels alone are not suitable for adobe blocks, as they do not have good adhesive properties, and will not stick together without another material as a binder, such as portland cement. Some gravels are excellent for filler material or as drains, but we may ignore them for adobe block manufacture.

SAND consists of fine grains of rock, mostly quartz types. The individual sand grains vary from about ¼″ to the smallest grain you can see without magnification. Sand may be found in streambeds, glacial areas, beaches, deserts, etc. If individual grains are too tiny to be distinguished with the unaided eye, the material is either silt or clay. In common with gravel, sand has no adhesive properties without the addition of a binding material. However, sandy clay or clayey sand both make excellent material for adobe blocks.

SILT is ground rock in which the individual grains are too tiny to be distinguished without magnification. Silt also has poor adhesive qualities, although it will tend to hold together when moistened and compressed. Silt may be found almost anywhere, as glacial deposits, in the beds of slow streams or slack waters, or as aeolian (wind-borne) deposits. Silt alone does not make a good adobe block material, as it does not compact well, and is highly susceptible to moisture, and may swell when soaked. With the addition of stabilizers, such as portland cement for sandy silts, lime for clayey silts, or emulsified asphalt for either, silts may be made to serve in the absence of better soil.

CLAY is an earthen material, hard when dry, sticky when wet. The individual grains are too fine to be distinguished by the naked eye. There are many varieties of clay, some of which will expand and shrink considerably through the wet-dry cycle, while others may not. Clays may be located in valleys near slowly-moving waters, in coastal plains, flood plains, or in fan-shaped deposits at mountain run-offs. Clays will compact well with the proper moisture content, but are very susceptible to shrinkage and cracking when drying, then expanding again when wet. However, most clays are quite strong when kept dry, and are a good choice for adobe blocks, if lime or emulsified asphalt is used as a stabilizer or waterproofing.

ORGANIC SOILS contain rotted or partially decomposed vegetable matter, and may have a stringy or spongy appearance. These soils often are very moist and may have a distinctive odor. They may be found where water has been standing for some time, as in swamps. Good agricultural topsoil is organic soil, and it may be excellent for growing things, but it is no good for adobe blocks. These soils are generally too spongy to compress well, and the decomposing material within it shall continue to rot, and you don't need a rotten wall.

Remember that these soil types are seldom found in the pure state, but are usually intermixed with one or more of the other types. You may describe such mixtures as a clay containing some sand as a "sandy clay," or a sandy material intermixed with less gravel as a "gravelly sand," and so forth.

The best natural soil for adobe blocks is a sandy clay containing almost equal parts of sand and clay. If you can't find such a mixture conveniently near your building site and are willing to work damn hard for an optimum material, you have only to mix sand and clay until you get the right proportions. However, for modern construction, we advocate the use of the proper stabilizer for waterproofing, even if it is not needed for strength.

Of course, the optimum location of your adobe block material is that which you will have to excavate from your building site to construct the home. Soil samples from your site will be necessary at any rate to determine your foundation design. If you feel that you can afford the expense more than the time you would have to spend to do it yourself, you can retain the services of a Soils Engineer or Soils Testing Laboratory. These experts can perform complete testing and analysis, and give you their recommendations and advice for a moderate fee. However, even a moderate fee takes some money away from the funds you must have to purchase items or services that you cannot provide. We will assume that you wish to save the money and do it yourself, and will outline simple methods and tests to guide you.

To collect your soil samples, you will need a dirt auger or a post hole digger, hand tools, sample bags, several canvas tarpaulins, a 6′ ruler or tape, and paper and pencils. At each sample location, first strip off any organic topsoil, and set it aside in a stockpile. Such soil is not good for adobe blocks, but is necessary for landscaping or lawns. Then start digging the sample hole, setting the removed material on one of your tarps. Each time the material shows any change in type, color, or other characteristic, measure the depth at which the change occurred, and start a separate pile. Unless you are planning a deep sidehill cut or extensive basement for your home, you may not have to go more than 6' to 8' deep in your sample holes. Again, you must make the decision, based upon your needs and what you find in the sample holes. Even the distance between test holes is variable. When you start, you will see how variable the soil on your site is, and adjust your hole spacing accordingly. The more uniform the layers of soil in a hole series, the farther apart they may be dug and still get good results. If you run into extreme variations in soil layers between holes, dig more holes closer together until a reasonable soil profile may be drawn.

It is therefore quite important to start your sampling with good records, so that you don't wind up with too many uncertainties. One simple method is to log every sample on graph paper in a letter-number code. That is, locate each test hole in relation to some major physical feature, such as your lot corner, a big tree or some other permanent point. Then, start off your holes as A, B, C, etc. For each soil sample from each hole, use 1, 2, 3, etc., and measure the depth at which each type started and stopped, and its general type. Thus, typical sample labels might read, B-2, 2½' to 4', silty clay, and B-3, 4' to 8', sand. Place all of each individual sample removed in your sample bags, label them, and set them aside for testing. Then, when sampling is completed, you will have a permanent log record of each sample's original position.

You should take enough samples so that you are certain that what you have reasonably reflects the actual soil conditions on your site. After you are satisfied on quantity and quality and have all the samples bagged, labeled and recorded, you are ready to begin a series of simple tests on each sample.

When testing sands or gravels, dry the sample by heating or spreading in the sun. Then, place the sample in a mounded pile, and divide it into four equal parts. Combine two diagonally opposite quarters into one, and set aside the remainder. If the split sample is then much larger than a shovelful, continue the splitting process until you get down to that quantity. This method will aid in obtaining a small test sample that is truly representative of the original quantity.

You can learn a good bit about a soil from these simple visual tests. Spread the dried sample thinly over a flat surface, and separate it into three piles by size. In the first pile, place all grains or particles over ¼" in size; this is gravel. In the second, place all individual grains less than ¼", yet large enough to distinguish with the naked eye; this is sand. The remainder will be a pile of powdery residue in which the individual grains cannot be detected without magnification; this is either silt or clay. The identity of the entire sample is that of the largest pile. For instance, if the gravel pile is the largest, with a smaller sand pile, followed by a tiny silt or clay pile, the sample is a sandy gravel with a trace of silt or clay. Record this observation with the sample identification code and proceed.

If the sample is basically sand or gravel, remix the material and moisten it. Mold handfuls into small balls and let them dry in the sun. If the balls lose shape and fall apart as they dry, you have a clean sand or gravel that will not be good adobe material without the addition of clay and/or a stabilizer. If the balls hold their shape as they dry and become hard, you have a dirty sand or gravel which, subject to further tests, may make a good adobe block material.

If the sample is primarily a silt or clay, or dirty sand or gravel, again remix the entire sample, and sift the fines; that is, the material smaller than about 1/64", through a very fine screen or coarse cloth, collect these fines and continue the tests.

Form a ball about egg size with these fines, and wet it just enough to hold the ball together without sticking to the fingers. Flatten the ball slightly in your palm, and tap the back of your hand against some firm object rapidly, until the vibration brings a sheen of water to the surface of the sample. Then, squeeze the sample slightly to see if the water sheen disappears. The sheen of water will appear, but the objective of this test is to determine whether it appears rapidly or slowly. If the sample requires only five to ten taps to bring out the water sheen, this is a rapid reaction, and slight squeezing of the sample should cause the sheen to disappear immediately. Continued squeezing may cause the sample to crack and crumble. This reaction is typical of very fine sands and coarse silts.

If the sample requires 20 to 30 taps to bring out the water sheen, this is a sluggish reaction, and squeezing the ball will make it flatten, not crack or break. This indicates the presence of clay, rather than silt. Indeed, some samples will show little or no water sheen reaction, no matter how long they are vibrated. Thus, the more sluggish the reaction, the more clay the sample contains. Again, record these observations with the sample code, as the data simply isn't worth a damn unless you can document all of it. Perhaps your memory is infallible, but it is not too likely.

The next series to be run is the "Thread" test. From your wet sample, mold a ball about the size of a large marble. Again, it should be just wet enough to mold easily without becoming sticky. Then, use the palm of your hand, rolling the ball against a flat surface to roll it into a thread. If the ball will not roll out into a thread, even when more water is added, and continually crumble, the sample does not contain clay, and is therefore sand or silt. If the ball threads out well, continue rolling until the thread is about 1/8″ in diameter. When the sample has the right moisture content, it will begin to separate into smaller segments. So keep on remolding and rolling until the thread begins to break up when it is at about ⅛″ diameter. When this state is achieved, remold the sample into a ball and squeeze it between thumb and forefinger.

The degree of pressure required to deform the ball indicates the amount of clay present, from very light pressure meaning more silt than clay, all the way up to very heavy pressure indicating mostly clay in the sample. If the ball reacts as spongy and soft, stringy or bouncy, the sample contains organic soil and is not suitable for adobe construction.

The next series to be run through is the "Dry Strength" test. From your sample, prepare a half dozen wet pats about 2″ in diameter and ½″ thick, with enough moisture content for the soil to be quite soft, but still firm enough to hold the shape of the pat. Dry these pats in the sun until they are dried completely through, then break each pat in your hands and try to powder it between your fingers. If the sample has high dry strength, it will be hard to break and will snap sharply. The soil will not powder between the fingers, although it may crumble a bit. This high dry strength is a characteristic of great clay content, and is very desirable if the right stabilizer or waterproofing agent is mixed into this soil for adobe blocks.

It will not be too hard to break a soil pat with medium dry strength and some pressure may powder the broken pat to individual grains. This indicates a soil which has high levels of both clay and sand, which should make excellent adobe blocks, with or without the addition of a strength stabilizer, although we feel that some waterproofing agent should always be included.

Soil pats with low dry strength will break and powder easily, and may crumble even without any pressure. This means the soil sample has a low clay content, and is high in sand or silt. Such soils should not be used without the addition of either more clay, or a stabilizer such as portland cement.

A good, short test for organic soils is smell. Freshly dug, or wet, heated organic soils have a musty odor. Again, we emphasize that you must not use organic soils in adobe construction. A soil that has rotting and decomposing matter in it will continue this action if put into an adobe wall, and there is no way you can stop it.

The "Bite" test can give quick identification of sand, silt and clay. Place a small pinch of the questionable soil between your teeth and grind lightly. Sandy soils have hard, sharp grains which will grate upon the teeth in an unpleasant manner. Silty soil grains are smaller than sand, and will also grate, but are smoother than sand. Clay soils are smooth and powdery between the teeth, rather than gritty.

The manner in which it washes off your hands may also reveal a bit about soil types. Clay soils feel slick and may be hard to wash off. Silty soils feel powdery and dusty, but wash off easily. Sandy soils are gritty, but rinse off with no effort.

As you perform these various tests upon all of your test samples, keep a complete record of all observations and decisions. You may think that testing the sample and deciding that the particular soil will or will not suffice for adobe blocks is adequate, but it will not be so. A complete record of all your soil test results and observations will prove invaluable, once they are logged by code and correlated to the sample locations. You will, or should, then have a complete soils profile showing the depth and extent of all soil types in the top 6' to 8' of your building site. Thus, in addition to getting the best type soil you have available to manufacture the adobe blocks, you also avoid blind excavation because you know or can interpolate what type soils will be encountered. Also, the material you have taken for samples may also be used to design the house's foundations. Don't throw these records away when you start the house construction, but file and keep them. Who knows what you may decide to add to your place in the future, a larger garage, a shop, more bedrooms, perhaps even a swimming pool. It's much easier to make file space for these records than to throw them away, then have to do all that tedious work all over again someday.

Don't let yourself get stampeded or confused by all of this soils data; take it slow and easy until you are sure of yourself, just play it calm and cool, and you'll do a good job in spite of yourself. If, for reasons of time or laziness, you really don't want to do all of this soils work, go out and retain a Soils Engineer or a Soils Testing laboratory. Be sure to tell them what data you want, and also why you want it, and they'll give you a complete, written report for a moderate fee. In this, as in all other decisions for your adobe home, we just set out the ways and means, the final decisions are always up to you alone.

CHAPTER III

Adobe Block Stabilization

The addition of the correct stabilizing material can make some presently unsuitable soils adequate for adobe block construction. In addition, it can make a good block soil into an excellent one. The primary functions of stabilizers, in this reference, is to glue the soil grains together to create a higher level of strength, to waterproof the blocks and wall to prevent absorption of water, and to keep the soil stable; i.e., prohibit or impede shrinkage and swelling.

Many of the historic deficiencies of adobe homes may be eliminated or considerably diminished by the addition of stabilizers. Water is about the greatest hazard to adobe. It erodes walls, cracks plaster, rots the base of walls, and in general thoroughly attacks any soil structure through erosion or rotting. A proper stabilizer added to the mix when the blocks are made, and also used in the mortar and plaster on the home, will waterproof all surfaces to aid in preventing water damage to the structure.

Due to the inherent varieties in soil types and properties, and almost the same variations in stabilizing agents, there is no one, set bromide solution to all stabilization problems. Therefore, as we will do throughout this book, we shall set forth some of the problems and offer alternate solutions, and let you make the final decision. After you have gone through this data and decided upon the stabilizer you wish to use to fit your soil conditions, you should make a series of test blocks, using different quantities of stabilizer in each batch, to see what the optimum quantity will be for your specific soil. This is important, as using too little stabilizer will not get the job done properly, and using too much is a pure waste of money.

As regards money, throughout this book we offer advice on how to do things yourself to avoid spending money. On adobe stabilizers, we advocate spending the money to purchase adequate stabilizing agents, as we feel that this expense produces benefits far outweighing the cost Certainly, some of the old-timers will tell you about the adobe house just down the road, which was built over two hundred years ago, and never even heard of stabilizers. That's absolutely true, but think of how many more times that house had to be patched, repaired, and replastered than if they had stabilizers available to them when it was built. Actually, some old adobes did have stabilizers in them, but they were not called that, it was just "something extra" that some wise old man put into the blocks.

So, the following paragraphs will discuss the common stabilizers, and what type soils need which stabilizing properties, so go to it.

SAND AND CLAY may both be considered as stabilizers under certain circumstances. A not unusual condition in soils is to discover that sands and clays are deposited in alternating layers under the topsoil. These layers may be quite variable, both in thickness and soil type. After you have performed your soil tests, you will know the rough proportions of the soils in each layer. As we have said, neither a pure sand nor clay make good adobe block material. However, a clayey sand or a sandy clay are excellent adobe soils. So, for either extreme, you mix the opposite soil into it thoroughly to manufacture a stabilized soil. Thus, by blending clay into sand, or vice versa, two unsuitable soils are changed, or stabilized, into one desirable material. It should be recognized that this blending may not be accomplished as easily as it sounds. Due to its excellent adhesive properties, clay may not be too easy to pulverize, especially when wet. The large lumps and clots must be broken up and the entire mass of sand and clay mixed thoroughly into one homogenous blend. This is very important with all stabilizers, to effect the desired results, they must be blended through-out the mass of the unstable soil. This mixing is a tremendous amount of hard labor if done by hand. A handy labor-saving method here is to buy or rent a small power concrete mixer, then put alternate shovels of the two soils into the rotating mixer, add the right amount of water, and place the mix directly into your adobe block forms. Even after you have a good blend of clay and sand, we highly recommend the addition of another suitable stabilizer to waterproof the blocks.

PORTLAND CEMENT is an often-used stabilizer with the sand or gravel soils. The addition of portland cement produces a mixture called Soil-Cement, which is stronger and more adhesive than the sand or gravel soils alone. The greater strength is beneficial, but there are some problems with this particular stabilizer. First, portland cement may cost from around $1.85 to $2.00 or more per 94 pound sack, and if your sandy-gravel soil should require 4% by weight of cement, that becomes a significant expense item. Also, portland cement starts a chemical reaction as soon as it is wet, and must be placed in the forms before it sets. If the mixture sets before it can be molded, it must be thrown away. Soil-Cement should be "cured" to develop its strength, or you have wasted its potential. One curing method is to cover the cast blocks with burlap, which is kept constantly wet for at least seven days, and preferably fourteen. Soil-Cement is relatively easy to mix, if a power concrete

mixer is used, and cast into the forms before the mass starts to harden, or set. This particular stabilizer increases adobe block resistance to water, but does not definitely waterproof unless the portland cement content is comparatively high.

LIME is a good stabilizer for clay soils. Either the slaked or unslaked lime may be used with equal effect on the clay stabilization, but the slaked or hydrated form is safer to handle. The unslaked or quicklime form is somewhat hazardous to use, as it will burn on contact to skin and may damage the lungs if its dust is inhaled. The addition of lime to a heavy clay soil will aid in reducing the stickiness of the clay, and also help to reduce the lumpiness and make the soil more workable. However, lime requires an even longer curing period than Soil-Cement, the blocks must be kept moist for at least 14 days, and should not be placed in the wall for from one to two months after the wet curing to permit full strength development. Lime as a stabilizer will make clay soils easier to work, but will not add any appreciable strength, nor will it waterproof the block. In some sandy soils with low clay content, a combination of lime and portland cement produces effective stabilization, but you must evaluate whether the benefits of this mix are worth the increase in both cost and labor.

ASPHALT, in its various forms, is one of the oldest and best of adobe block stabilizers. Analyses of some ancient adobe homes dating from before the time of Nebuchadnezzar, who was King of Babylon about 600 B.C., indicate that natural asphalts were used as stabilizers in their adobe mixes. Asphalt in its basic state is a very heavy, thick oil, which will not blend well into other materials without heating. As such heating is not too practical for adobe block making, the asphalt is mixed with diluting materials so as to render it thinner and more workable. The two main varieties of these diluted asphalts are cutbacks and emulsions, both of which are readily available on the commercial market.

Cutback Asphalts have been diluted with gasoline, kerosene or one of the other light volatile petroleum derivatives. Cutbacks are not as desirable in adobe as emulsions, as the volatiles used to dilute the asphalt must be allowed to evaporate after mixing with the soil. This requires spreading the mixture to dry before it is molded into blocks. Aside from the additional time and labor, the use of cutback asphalts creates a definite fire hazard, and we do not recommend their use if other solutions are available.

Asphalt Emulsions are asphalt diluted with water, and to us, are the most suitable stabilizers for appropriate adobe soils. As the adobe block cures, the emulsion separates into asphalt and water. The water evaporates and leaves the asphalt as a thin film coating the grains of soil. This asphalt film coating acts as both a binder and as an excellent waterproofing agent. Emulsions are highly suitable for almost all adobe soils except those with an extremely high clay content, as the clay may not permit the asphalt to coat its individual grains as well as do the sands or gravels. However, such soils may be corrected by adding sand to the mix to diminish the percentage of clay.

Another benefit of asphalt emulsions is the comparative ease of their blending into the adobe material. Depending upon the exact type of your soil, the proper quantity of asphalt emulsion may range somewhere around ten percent by volume of the water added to the soil. As with all other stabilizers, this will have to be determined by testing various mixes in actual blocks, and selecting the best result for the least cost. We recommend the use of a small power concrete mixer to ease the mixing labor and speed up the process. Asphalt emulsion may be added directly into the mixing water, as by pouring the amount of required emulsion into a clean container, then filling it with water. For instance, to produce a 10% mix, use a clean 55 gallon oil drum, pour in 5½ gallons of emulsion, fill the drum with water, then add the drum contents into the concrete mixer as needed to make a workable adobe soil to cast into the forms. With some adobe soils, asphalt emulsion stabilizers give such excellent strong, waterproof blocks that an exterior plaster is not really necessary, except for aesthetics.

Some people may feel that an unplastered adobe block wall has an attractive roughhewn look, but we prefer the traditional plaster for all exterior surfaces. However, some interior walls are very decorative when unplastered, only whitewashed or painted.

STRAW has long been a traditional additive in adobe blocks, but produces little benefit compared to adequate stabilization. The only real benefit from straw is the minor easing of water evaporation in heavy clay soils while the blocks are curing, and thus slightly aids the prevention of contraction cracking. Straw very slightly increases the strength of wet adobe blocks, but actually decreases the strength of the dry, cured block. Also, straw will permit the absorption of water into a finished wall, deteriorating it. To us, straw has no value at all in adobe blocks, if any other stabilizer is available.

FLY-ASH AND LIME have had some good results as an adobe stabilizer. Fly-Ash is the fine dust which is the residue from the burning of solid fuels such as coal or coke. When blended with lime in proportions of three or four parts of fly-ash to one part of lime, this results in a stabilizer almost as strong as portland cement, at a lower cost. Fly-Ash may be available at little or no cost as a waste product of factories or power plants burning fossil fuels; if one is in your vicinity, check on the availability of this additive.

SODIUM SILICATE, often called "waterglass," creates a waterproof coating with durable qualities on sandy-soil adobe blocks. This material is not a true stabilizer, but a coating agent, as it is added to the surface of the finished block, rather than being mixed into the soil before the block is cast. The sodium silicate is utilized as a dip, by mixing about one part of it with three parts of water in a large container, then immersing each block in the solution at least twice, for about one minute each time. The blocks, when cured for 7 days, have a hard, waterproof coating. However, if the material has not penetrated to an adequate depth, the coating is susceptible to damage from handling during building, and may result in weak spots. This coating is excellent if well done, but does require a separate operation, and therefore greater cost in time and labor.

A great many other substances have been used as adobe block stabilizers, with varying benefits and cost. These have included such wide variations as tannic acid, resins, sulfites, cattle urine or dung, molasses, some vegetable oils, and almost anything else that men could dream up. So if you have some pet idea, test it in a series of blocks and see what happens. In general, we recommend asphalt emulsion as an optimum solution for most soils and locations, but this may not be best in all cases. Due to unique characteristics of your soil, or the availability of other products, perhaps from your employment or location, something else may give equal or better results at a lower cost. So try it out, and use whatever is best for you.

Again, time spent in planning and testing always pays off in actual results. After you have examined your needs and tested your soils, you will have a pretty good idea of what you need and want in stabilizers. The only way to accurately determine the quantity of a specific stabilizer that is optimum for your soil is to make a series of test blocks. These blocks should be made to the same size that you intend to use in your home, both to assure proper testing conditions and to avoid wasting good blocks. The mix proportions must be varied through the test block series,

from quite small amounts of stabilizer to large quantities. Some authorities recommend a series of ten blocks, with the stabilizer increased proportionately through the series. We do not feel that this quantity will always give definitive results, as there are other things that can make a block fail besides stabilizer adequacy. Two or three blocks at least should be made for each varied mix, to provide enough data for a valid crosscheck.

Again, keep full records of all of this testing in a permanent form. Write down all the variations of mixes, and mark the block with a number code, so that you can positively identify the mix that went into each separate block. It is quite useless to have an adobe block that you decide is the best of the series, if you can't remember exactly what went into it, and in what proportions. All of the adobe blocks placed into your home should be as uniform in mix as is possible. If you change mixes, or get sloppy in your work, you will introduce severe uncertainties into the completed work. Also, both the mud mortar to bind the blocks together, and the mud plaster used to cover the wall surface should be of the same mix as the adobe blocks themselves.

So, hurrah, you at long last have developed the best low cost mix for your adobe soil and stabilizer, and are now ready to start the back-breaking labor of making perhaps several thousand adobe blocks.

CHAPTER IV

Adobe Blocks

Now begins the heavy work, as you should be about ready to start up your adobe block factory. Yet again, good planning and organizing will avoid a great deal of unnecessary labor. You now have your soil source, have tested the soil, decided upon the stabilizer to use, and have arrived at the optimum mixture for your adobe blocks. If you are lucky, your adobe soil source is on your building site, and thus will eliminate the additional labor of transporting either the soil or the completed blocks to the home-site.

Again, you have a decision to make if your soil site is not near the home-site. That is, where do you set up your block-making operation? This decision hinges primarily upon the availability of each area, and the comparative problems involved in transporting either the raw materials or the cured blocks. In most cases, it may be easier to haul the adobe soils to your building site and make your blocks right where they will be used. For convenience, we will assume that your adobe soils are available upon your building site. So all you have to do is dig it out and stockpile it for the block-making operation. This also sounds very simple, but then nothing in this life is ever as easy as it can be made to sound.

From your soil testing records, you should have a good knowledge of the depth and extent of the soil or soils that you will use in the blocks. From the best area, first strip off all the topsoil, and put it in an out-of-the-way stockpile for later use. Then, dig out your selected soils, and place them in one or more stockpiles right at the area where you will be making the blocks. Plan this work area so that you don't have to do any extra shoveling and hauling. One method is to lay out the work area like a wheel, mixing area in the hub, and soil stockpiles, block forming and curing points as the spokes. Be sure to plan this area large enough, so that you have room to work and move without falling over everything.

If you will have to mix soils to get good adobe material, we recommend that you place these soils in separate stockpiles as you dig them out. Some authorities say to mix them as you remove them from the ground, but we do not feel that this will produce uniform results. Excavation with a backhoe or endloader will save a lot of hand labor during this stockpiling, but these machines may be overly expensive on either contract or rental costs, so once again, it's up to you whether you need to save labor or money. Either way, it's going to be a lot of work, as you will need what may come to seem an enormous lot of soil. Depending upon wall thickness and height, and the density of the blocks, it may require from 500 pounds to almost a ton of adobe soil per foot of wall length.

In the design of your adobe home, you will establish the wall thickness, height of wall, and total length of adobe wall, so multiply these three figures to determine the total cubic feet of adobe blocks in the home. Then determine the cubic area of one of your adobes, and divide the total volume of the walls by this figure to establish the minimum number of blocks needed.

This number should be increased by 15% to 20% to allow for breakage, errors, etc. Multiplying the number of blocks by the weight of an average block will give you the rough total of pounds of soil, or, before you have the blocks to weigh, an approximate total may be obtained by multiplying the total cubic feet by 0.05, resulting in tons of soil required. These are only approximate figures, but even so, don't let their magnitude scare you, we told you it was going to be a lot of work.

By whatever means you excavate (dig) your soil, it will contain some clods or lumps, and perhaps rocks or trash, which must all be either broken down or removed. Therefore, your soils must be screened, either before or after stockpiling. It may be more practical to do this as you stockpile the soils, simply to have it done with and more room to work in later on. You will need a large, durable screen, preferably metal, in which the openings are the size of the largest bits of soil you want in your mix, generally from ¼" to ½". This screen is mounted on legs or braces at an angle of from 45 to 60 degrees to the ground surface in a clear work area. Then shovel your soils against the upper surface of the screen, and the small bits will go through and the large clods, lumps, rocks, etc., will slide to the base of the screen. The lumps may be broken up to go back through the screen, and the rocks and other trash may be discarded. You now have one or more stockpiles of screened adobe soil, so sit down and take a breather.

We now assume that you have all materials stockpiled; i.e., soil of one or two types, stabilizer, water, and your block forms. Here we get into another point of contention, as it seems that there are almost as many recommended sizes for adobe blocks as there are block-makers. An adobe block can, and undoubtedly has, been made to almost any conceivable set of dimensions, but remember that the block has to fit into your wall, and that you will have to lift and place each and every one of them. Therefore, the weight of the block should be low enough so that continued lifting them is not unduly tiring, without making them so small as

to increase the work of laying them in place. So, as you may have already guessed, here comes another decision that you will have to make. As we have said before, we do not feel that an adobe wall less than two feet thick produces all the structural, insulating and aesthetic values of the traditional adobe home. In our opinion, the ideal adobe block size for this 24" nominal wall thickness is one which is 12" long by 8" wide and 4" thick. Depending upon soil densities, stabilizer, etc., a block this size may weigh from 20 to 30 pounds. This combination requires two blocks per transverse, or crosswise laid courses, and three blocks per longitudinal, or lengthwise laid courses. Coursing, or the method of alternating block layers, will be fully discussed in the wall-laying section, but we touch lightly upon it here, as many so-called authorities completely ignore it, and it does seriously affect either wall thickness, stability or optimum block size.

If you adopt a different wall thickness, you can go to several different proportions on block sizes. For the same proportions as that above; i.e., a 2/3 block wall, make each block one-half the wall thickness in length, and one-third the wall thickness in width. Or, you may decide upon a ½ block wall, wherein each block is the full wall thickness in length, and one-half the wall thickness in width. If you decide to build a comparatively thin wall, you may even make the blocks the full wall thickness in width, and anything you can lift in length. For any nominal block size, make the forms so that the actual size of the block is about ⅛" less than plan size, to allow for mortar and to thus keep the wall in constant dimensions. Therefore, a nominal 12 x 8 x 4 block will actually measure 11⅞" x 7⅞" x 3⅞". Of course, if you have decided to purchase your adobe blocks instead of making them, you will have to take what is available on the market, and this entire chapter becomes redundant.

Having decided upon the block size, you now make the forms in which the blocks are to be cast. These forms must be sturdily built, as they are going to incur considerable wear and tear throughout the block-making operation. 2 x 4 lumber is a good choice if a 4″ thick block is desired. The lumber should be grade 1 or 2 common, so as to avoid warps, large knots or other defects. Use screws, bolts or metal corner reinforcing to hold the form sections rigidly together, to make the forms strong enough to produce uniform blocks. As the forms will be almost constantly wet, treat the wood with oil or some other preservative. You might even line the inner surfaces of the form with tin, a light sheet metal, or other material to increase its durability and to ease the form's removal from the cast blocks.

For average-size adobe blocks, we recommend making your forms so that each unit will cast four blocks. Larger form units have been utilized for commercial adobe block manufacturing, but are too heavy and cumbersome for limited manpower to handle. Make up four or five sets of these four-block units so as to permit production at a reasonable rate. Don't try to get too ambitious on the soil volumes you may tackle in a single mixing, as you will have to cast, rod and compact each block, and finish each top surface before the mixture starts to dry and set up. Start small, and work up to a comfortable volume that you can utilize without rushing the work, or wasting mixed material. The form units will be open on both top and bottom, so that the units may be lifted off the cast blocks without damaging them. Therefore, to achieve an acceptable surface on the block bottoms, the forms must be placed upon a smooth, even surface for the casting operation. This surface may be the concrete slab for your house floor, sheets of plywood, or even a cleared, level, hard ground area. A rough, dirty form site will result in uneven, marred adobe blocks which will cause some serious problems when attempting to lay the wall courses.

The most ancient known method for mixing soils for adobe blocks is the "wet-pit." In a shallow depression in the ground, the soils were shoveled in, water was added, and the mass was mixed with feet, hands, rakes, hoes, shovels, or anything else available. The mixing was continued until the mass was somewhat uniform,

then it was carried to the forms, and cast into blocks. Quite often, the ground depression used was the point the adobe soils had been dug from in the first place. Regrettably, this method is still in use today in some areas, and even yet is advocated by some who should know better. Aside from the huge amount of hand-labor required, it is almost impossible by this means to get a homogenous mixture of the batch, nor is it feasible to reproduce the same batch proportions, mix after mix. These irreconcilable variations can introduce severe defects into your block walls, the true effect of which may sadly be learned over the years in residence.

We strongly recommend the utilization of a powered rotary mixer, such as is commonly rented or sold for mixing portland cement concrete. These mixers are available in several sizes, to suit your particular demands. If, as is increasingly normal, you are working alone or with very little manual assistance, the ¼ cubic yard capacity unit should be adequate. Such a mixer will not only save needless hand labor, but will also speed up the operation, permit flexibility in use, and will aid in uniformity and quality control.

As the prime result of your soil testing, you have already adopted the optimum mix proportions for your soil or soils and the selected stabilizer. If your chosen mix is good, the only variation you should permit from this point on is the amount of water, which may vary a bit due to changes in moisture content of the soil as you use it. Once again, organize your working area efficiently. Plan it out ahead, so that you have room to work without stumbling over things, and also without having to fetch and carry very far. Place the rotary mixer near the soil stockpiles, and arrange the clean water supply and stabilizer close to the mixer. Locate the form area a bit further away, with plenty of open space near to the forms, as the blocks will have to stay in the same position after the forms are lifted, so you will need space to relocate the forms some few times. To clean the forms after each casting, you will also need a second water supply near the form area. Don't use your mixing water for form-cleaning, as the dirty water will introduce uncertainties into the mix proportions, and impede good quality control. You will also need shovels, buckets, a wheelbarrow, a short rod of wood or metal, a trowel or straightedge, and of course, extra fuel for the mixer, if it has a gas engine. There also is the prime component of your adobe home, lots of sweat and muscle.

After all these tedious preparations, at last begins the actual production of adobe blocks. Start up the rotary mixer, and with shovel or bucket, place the first measured load of soil into the mixer. If your stabilizer is a dry powder, such as portland cement concrete or lime, add the correct quantity to the mixer with the dry soil. If the stabilizer is liquid, such as asphalt emulsion, it should already be mixed in the selected proportions into the water. Then, add the least amount of water required for your mix, which can only be determined by trying, testing and working. With most mixes, about one minute of rotary mixing after the water is added will be enough time to produce a well-blended batch. Discharge the mixer batch into the wheelbarrow, and take it to the form area to cast the adobe blocks.

Don't just dump the wheelbarrow load into the form unit, but fill each block by hand or with a trowel, by casting each blob into the form with a bit of force. Jab a rod or trowel repeatedly into the block to consolidate the mass, so as to eliminate air bubbles or voids, and to help assure block solidity, with strong corners and edges. Then, put the top finish on each block by drawing a trowel or straightedge over the top surface of the form to remove excess material, and smooth out the top of the block with the trowel. A few drops of water sprinkled across the block may help the trowel produce a smooth, even block face, but don't use too much water, it may weaken the block.

After you have filled, rodded and finished all of your block form units, and have used all of the mixed batch, let the blocks start to set or dry, and remove the form units by lifting them straight up off the blocks. Here yet again is a point that may be decided only by you after try-

ing; i.e., the time the cast block will need to start to set before you can remove the form. This time period is influenced by so many factors, soil type, moisture content, stabilizer used, casting time, and even weather, that it is impossible to predict without some experimentation. When the forms are removed, if the blocks slump or bulge, it is either too soon or the mix is too wet. If the mix sticks to the forms, it is either too late, the mix is too dry, or the forms have not been oiled properly. With very little practice at this, you will become quite expert at timing the form removal. Remember to be careful when lifting the forms up from the blocks, it won't pay to go through all the labor of mixing and casting, only to break the blocks by careless form removal.

Immediately after lifting the forms from the cast blocks, clean and wash the form units thoroughly, so that there is no material clinging on them to ruin the next batch. Relay the form units on the prepared surface next to the just-cast blocks, return to go, and start the mixing and casting operation all over again. Long before you have manufactured all the blocks you need, you may feel that you can perform this entire cycle in your sleep, and you may be correct, as there is no denying that it is a long, hard, boring job.

When using a lime or portland cement stabilizer, the blocks must be covered and kept moist for at least seven days, and in some cases, preferably for fourteen days. For such blocks, right after removing the forms, cover the blocks with burlap, straw, or some other porous material, wet it down, and keep the covering moist for the entire curing period. After the moist curing period is completed, turn the blocks up on edge to finish off the cure.

For most other stabilizers, you may turn the blocks up on edge to cure as soon as they are strong enough to handle without damage. This may be anywhere from two to four days after casting. For the curing period, set the blocks up on edge, each far enough apart so that air may circulate freely between them. Yet again, the curing period depends upon your existing conditions and the block components, although most authorities agree upon at least one month. If there is a chance of the blocks being rained upon during this period, erect some type of shelter to protect them, perhaps only a tarp hung on posts over the blocks.

After the curing is done, the blocks may be piled or stacked near the home, to await their use in the walls. Don't feel that you must make the entire quantity of blocks in one long, grinding, continuous operation. It's a terrific amount of work, and you may wish to alternate the job to avoid tedium. Suit yourself, after all, it's your home and you are the only final judge of how and when you will get things done. You may wish to excavate all of the required soil at once, just to get it over, or perhaps in stages, as dig, make blocks, dig again, and on and on, ad infinitum, ad nauseum.

Whether you make all the blocks at once, or in stages, don't ignore your total needs. After calculating the number of blocks you will need to build the house, add at least 15% to 20% onto the top figure to allow for breakage, errors, etc. It will be a good deal more convenient to spend some extra time making more blocks than you figure to need, than to have the home almost done and have to stop building to go back to block-making. As we keep harping upon, plan, plan, and yet again, plan.

Also just because this book is laid out in a certain order of chapters, don't feel that each item of work must be performed in the sequence we have written it. Each segment is a part of the whole, and does not stand alone. Certain operations must be done in order; i.e., soil samples and tests must be done before blocks may be made, and the home size and wall thickness must be decided before the foundation may be designed, etc. But there are a few things you may do in the order you wish, as you may build the foundation before, during, or after the block manufacturing. Try not to consider a single operation by itself, rather how it relates to the whole. Many of the chapters of this book require action relating to a separate chapter, as plumbing, heating and wiring must all be considered when building the foundation, floors and walls. So yet again, read the entire book, study your needs and alternatives, make all the major, and most of the minor decisions as soon as you can, and plan, plan, plan.

CHAPTER V

Foundations

The foundation of your adobe home is the base upon which it stands, the source of the home's strength and stability. Even the very best of construction throughout the rest of the home shall ultimately fail, if the foundation is not adequate. An undersized or poorly built foundation will become unstable, shift or break, and torque the house walls and floors, causing cracking leading to major deterioration. In severe cases, foundation subsidence has collapsed walls and entire homes. Thus, the foundation is the most important single element of your home, and deserves serious planning, good preparation, and careful construction.

Adobe homes, because of their massive walls and comparatively great weight, require more substantial foundations in most soils than do light-weight houses, such as frame construction. It is a rather curious fact that many homeowners can answer almost any question about their home's dimensions and construction criteria, with the glaring exception of foundation data. He may be able to reel off reams of data on his home's wall thickness and material, stud or rafter spacing, size of most other components, but ask him the depth and area of his foundation footing, and he most often answers only with a perplexed expression. The general reaction may be to ignore it, it's mostly down below the ground, so forget it and maybe it won't go away. If an older house has stood for some few years without major wall cracking, you might ignore the foundation, except for looking every few years to be sure it hasn't been stolen.

But that just isn't good enough for your new adobe home, so we will once again sally forth on a dissertation of whys and wherefores about foundation generalities, give you the doubtful benefit of our advice, then, as usual, leave the final decision to you. A typical oversimplification would be to state that the basic purpose of a foundation is to hold up the house. As far as this statement goes, it is somewhat correct. However, the major functions of a home foundation include transferring the weight of the home to the underlying soil in a manner that will not overload the bearing capacity of that soil; acting as a level, rigid base upon which to erect walls and floors; and to withstand lifting or twisting forces working against the house, such as severe winds or earth movements.

Foundations may consist of several different configurations, such as foundation walls bearing upon a continuous spread footing, or as beams or girders supported by pilings or piers. The piling or pier method is most often utilized where a considerable separation, or span distance, is required between support points. This method is exemplified by such wide extremes as a large bridge crossing a wide river or gorge, or the little palm-thatched hut, so dear to the South Sea Island movie clichés, which is raised off the ground upon tree-trunk piles. The distinction between piles and piers is probably irrelevant to this book, but we may as well set it forth for your edification. A pile is a long, slender object, usually of steel, concrete, or wood, which is driven by mechanical means into the soil until it either rests upon solid rock or attains its bearing capacity, wherein the friction between the soil and the pile resists the weight load imposed on the pile. A pier is also most often long and slender, made of steel, concrete or wood, but it is placed or built upon its base, which may be solid rock or a spread footing, or at times, may rest upon driven piles. Such foundations are almost never used under adobe homes.

The foundation method most applicable to adobe homes is the foundation wall atop a spread footing. This system is utilized to uniformly spread fairly heavy loadings over a continuous, limited area. It is typified by such diverse usages as large dams, culverts, canals, and homes. In this style foundation, the spread footing is designed to distribute the weight loading of the home over a larger area, so that the bearing capacity of the soil is not exceeded. That is, the foundation wall may be two feet wide, and the house may have a loading at the base of the wall of a ton per foot of length, thus creating a load at the base of the foundation wall of 1,000 pounds per square foot. Perhaps this particular soil may only sustain loadings of 500 pounds per square foot, therefore, the spread footing under the foundation wall will have to be four feet or more in width. Thus, the size of the spread footing is derived from the weight imposed; i.e., the weight of the entire home, and the bearing capacity of the underlying soil. Yet again, this is another decision that you must either make yourself, or consult a professional to give advice as to proper footing dimensions.

Different soils will not sustain the same loadings, as each soil strata has a definite bearing value, which must not be exceeded or the structure may fail. The strength, or bearing capacity of the soil immediately under the bottom elevation of the spread footing must be determined to design the footing. As extreme generalities, shallow clays or silts may perhaps bear less than 2,000 pounds per square foot, while some dense sands or gravels may sustain as much as 6,000 pounds per square foot. Also, the founding soil; i.e., the soil strata under the spread footing, should be uniform throughout the entire area

underling the home. If the soil changes type or grade under the planned homesite, relocate the home. This is easier and much safer to do, than to locate a foundation bearing upon an unstable soil transition area. Such a location is almost guaranteed to cause future problems regarding foundation stability, so avoid it.

Before you can determine the size of the footing, its location and elevation must be resolved. You have already chosen a site for the home, perhaps because of the view, the proximity of utilities, or even that it's the only place it will fit upon your lot because of the legal requirements on setbacks, etc. Having already performed the soil sampling and testing, you therefore know what type of soil lies at varying depths on the site, and have selected a location where the soil under the home will be uniform in character. The elevation of the footing may be affected by the geographic location of the home. If the home is to be built in temperate or arctic zones, that is, where seasonal weather changes create freezing and thawing cycles, the footing must lie below the frost line. If not, the freeze-thaw cycle may cause the footing to shift, and damage the home. The frost line is the depth to which the ground becomes frozen during an average or a record cold, winter. If this depth is not known to you, it can be checked with local authorities, such as a County Agent, the Farm Bureau, or even local builders. But determine this depth, then plan the entire footing below it.

If the home is to be located in a tropic zone, where a freeze-thaw cycle does not occur, the footing must still be placed deep enough to avoid changing surface conditions. These include agricultural topsoil, moisture variations, flooding-silt zones, etc. In these areas, a test hole may reveal a change in soil character, perhaps from loose, unconfined silts to a dense, more stable clay or sand at a depth of several feet below the surface. Plan the footing down into the stable area.

Now that the location and depth of the spread footing have been ascertained, the bearing strength of the soil under the footing must be tested. Perhaps the easiest, most accurate way to accomplish this bearing value test is to retain a Soils Engineer or Soils Testing Laboratory, who would perform the entire test for a modest fee. But any fee costs money, and you may prefer to do it yourself, yet again. The following paragraphs and accompanying illustrations will set forth a simple method for testing the bearing strength of your founding soil.

The first item of business is to make the simple "Lever Soil Tester" shown in the illustration. The only materials required are a 2 x 4, 6′ 2″ long, a 2 x 6 the same length, a wood block 3″ thick and 3¼″ square, and a piece of 8 or 10 gauge wire about two feet long. Assemble the Tester, place it in a cleared-off work area near the foundation site, and get the soil samples.

To obtain the bearing test soil samples, dig several test holes in the foundation area, down to the elevation of the proposed bottom of the spread footing. Space these test holes out around the complete foundation area, so that the samples will be truly representative of the average soil conditions to be encountered under the footing. Then, cut out four or more soil blocks from the bottom of each test hole. These soil blocks should then be trimmed to 3″ square by 6″ long. All work on or around these soil samples should be quite careful, so as to avoid breaking the samples before testing. You should obtain at least ten, and perhaps as many as twenty of the soil sample blocks to provide enough testing data to determine an accurate, average bearing strength. In fact, the bigger the home is to be, the more samples you should take. Throw away any soil blocks that become cracked or damaged in handling, as a flawed sample will give only flawed results.

Your assembled "Lever Soil Tester" should have all the letter points shown on the illustration scaled off and labeled. Place the first soil block sample on the 2x6 at point "A," put the small wood block on top of the sample, and gently lower the 2x4 down to rest upon the block. Then, press down on the "A" point on top of the 2x4 with one finger, to a pressure of 18 to 20 pounds. If you are not a good judge of weight or pressure,

practice this a bit on a scale, even a bathroom scale. If the soil block does not fail with this pressure at point "A," move your finger to point "B," without disturbing the test setup, and apply the same pressure at point "B." If the sample still has not failed, continue this pressure process down the letter scale until it does, and record the letter point at which it failed on your log sheet. Don't rush this testing, but do it carefully and diligently for all of the soil blocks, then check the average results. The blocks should all have failed near the same point for uniform character soils. If they did not average out well, check why not, as this could mean trouble, indicating variation in bearing strength through the footing area.

If the tests averaged well, obtain the letter point at which the majority of samples failed, say point "D," then, look in the footing dimension table under the next lower letter, in this case, "C," and find that for a 24″ thick wall over this soil, the spread footing should be 40″ wide and 12″ thick. In all cases, note the average letter point of failure, then take the footing dimensions from the table under the next lower letter. Of course, if all blocks failed at point "A," forget it, you don't want a home on that soft stuff without professional advice. Also, if you had done as we suggest, and read and studied all of this book before you started any work, you could have done this bearing strength testing at the same time you did the adobe block soil tests. Then you would have had all of this tedious testing behind you, and would be ready to start the actual construction of the footing and foundation wall.

The footing should be built from materials that will resist decay or insects, and that has inert qualities and good strength. Some authorities recommend stone, brick, concrete block or even soil-cement, but we feel that only portland cement concrete should be used as a cast foundation footing. In addition to possessing all the required resistance and strength characteristics, portland cement concrete also has the virtue of easy and rapid replacement. Concrete will perhaps cost more than other materials in actual

SIMPLE METHOD FOR INVESTIGATING STRENGTH OF ADOBE SOILS

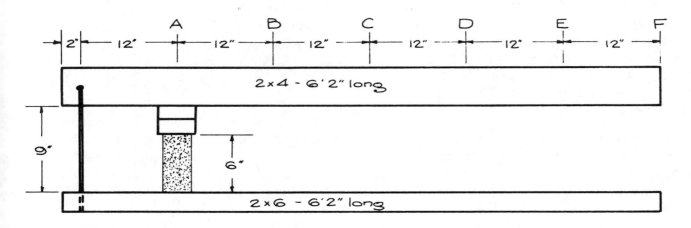

LEVER SOIL TESTER

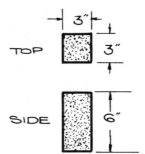

TRIM SOIL BLOCKS
FOR TESTING

PRESS AGAINST SUCCESSIVE LETTER POINTS UNTIL TEST BLOCK FAILS. USE PRESSURE OF 18 to 20 POUNDS WITH ONE FINGER OR OTHER CONCENTRATED WEIGHT.

USE MINIMUM OF 4 GOOD TESTS TO ESTABLISH THE AVERAGE FAILURE POINT.

TAKE FOOTING DIMENSIONS FROM TABLE UNDER NEXT LOWER LETTER BELOW AVERAGE FAILURE POINT. IF AVERAGE FAILURE AT "C", USE "B", ETC.

TYPICAL FOOTING DIMENSIONS IN ADOBE SOILS

SOIL STRENGTH	A		B		C		D		E		F	
WALL THICKNESS	W	T	W	T	W	T	W	T	W	T	W	T
12	36	8	24	10	18	12	15	12	12	12	12	12
15	36	10	30	10	24	11	20	12	18	12	18	12
18	40	12	36	12	30	12	24	12	24	12	24	12
24	48	18	48	12	40	12	36	12	36	12	30	12

NOTE: ALL DIMENSIONS SHOWN ARE IN INCHES, AND ARE AVERAGE REQUIREMENTS FOR SINGLE STORY STRUCTURES WITH EARTHEN ROOFS.

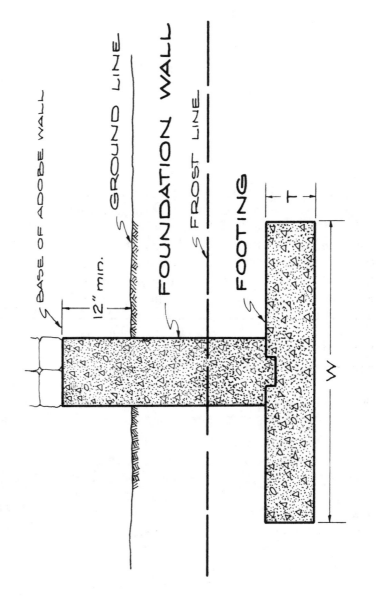

cash outlay, but we feel that this is more than offset by its advantages in strength, ease and time-saving.

Here yet again, you must make a choice. You may purchase ready-mix concrete delivered to the site from your local plant, or you can buy sacks of portland cement, stockpile sand and gravel, and mix your own concrete batches. We won't estimate the cost per cubic yard of ready-mix concrete for you, as factors of inflation, haul distance, material availability, and business competition will determine the price delivered to your site. You will have to investigate the cost for delivery of a specific concrete mix to your site, not just the general locality, then judge this cost against the value of your time and sweat expended in doing it yourself. If you do decide to roll your own, the concrete mixer that we advocated for the adobe block process was designed for the mixing of portland cement concrete. If you don't use the rotary mixer, you may have to make a large mortar box to mix the batches in, and this takes hand-mixing, which is a whole lot of sweat and backache, and can not produce concrete as uniformly as the rotary mixer, so use one.

Mixing your own concrete is not unduly complicated, if you follow the same procedures throughout to assure the production of uniform quality batches. The Portland Cement Concrete Tables herein set forth proportions for several mixes and quantities of concrete. These proportions are averages, and may require a little adjustment to fit your actual conditions; if you have a pet mix that you know produces good results, go ahead and use it. Although, once you have established a mix for a particular use, don't change anything except perhaps the amount of water while you are pouring the item. The right amount of water may vary because of changes in moisture content in the sand or gravel, so keep your mix as stiff, that is, as dry, as you can readily work it. Too much water makes lousy concrete.

Now, we'll take you through the motions to make a batch of concrete. We'll assume that you are going to pour a footing, will use the 3:5 mix, have a quarter-yard mixer, and the

sand is wet, but not soaked. In the table for material quantities for one cubic yard of concrete, you divide everything by four, since you are making a quarter-yard batch. Start up the mixer, and shovel into it about 3¾ cubic feet of sand and 5½ cubic feet of gravel, then add 1⅛ sacks of portland cement, and pour in just a bit over six gallons of water, and let the mixer revolve for one full minute. Remember, the water always goes in last. Then pour the batch either directly into the forms, or dump it into the wheelbarrow to haul to the forms, so save labor and mix near the forms. If you are satisfied with the results, start all over and keep going until the form is filled. This should be a two or three man operation for best results, as if you are working alone, the concrete first deposited may start to set up and harden before you can complete the pour.

However, before you can start a concrete pour, you have to have something ready to pour into. Forms must be built and erected to contain almost all concrete pours, so as to hold the mass to the desired lines and grades. Wherever the concrete will be exposed to view, the forms must have a quite smooth interior surface, as the concrete will naturally assume the shape and texture of the surface against which it is cast. Thick plywood is the usual interior form for such use, although special metal forms are also used. For work that will not be visible, lumber is adequate for forms, as a slightly rough surface will not matter. All formwork shall be rigid and well-braced, both to withstand the weight of the concrete, and to maintain straight, even lines in the cast mass.

Some foundation footings may be cast without forming, if the soil is stiff enough to be cut to the proper lines and grades without any sliding or crumbling. It will be easy to determine this while you are digging the footing area, and if you have any doubts at all, use forms. Excavate all the soil from the footing area, right down to the elevation of the bottom of the footing, being sure to dig out enough extra space around the planned footing area to leave room to move and work. Level off the bottom of the excava-

PORTLAND CEMENT CONCRETE

CONCRETE MIX PROPORTIONING

KIND OF WORK	CEMENT, SACKS	SAND, CU. FT.	GRAVEL, CU. FT.	GALS. WATER / SACK IF SAND IS:			MAX. GRAVEL SIZE
				DAMP	WET	SOAKED	
Footings, walls, Columns, below ground items	1	3	5	7	6	5	1½"
Floors, Tanks, Drives, Walks, watertight	1	2½	3½	6½	5	4½	1½"
Thin concrete, 2"-4" thk, posts decorative items	1	2	2	4½	3¾	3½	½"

APPROXIMATE MATERIAL QUANTITIES FOR ONE CUBIC YARD of CONCRETE

MATERIALS	MIX PROPORTIONS		
	1:2:2	1:2½:3½	1:3:5
CEMENT, Sacks	8	6	4½
SAND, Cubic Feet	16	15	15
GRAVEL, Cu. Ft.	16	21	22

1 bag of Cement = 1 Cu. Ft., 94 lbs.   1 Ton of Sand or Crushed Stone = ± 22 c.f.

4 bags of Cement = 1 Barrel   1 Ton of Gravel = ± 20 cubic feet

APPROXIMATE MATERIAL QUANTITIES FOR 100 SQUARE FEET of CONCRETE

PROPORTIONS	1:2:2			1:2½:3½			1:3:5			Yield, cu. yd. of Conc.
SLAB THICKNESS, INCHES	Cement, bags	Sand, cu. ft.	Gravel, cu. ft.	Cement, bags	Sand, cu. ft.	Gravel, cu. ft.	Cement, bags	Sand cu. ft.	Gravel, cu. ft.	
3	6½	16	16	5½	13¾	19½	4¼	12¾	21	~1
4	8½	21¼	21¼	7½	18¾	26	5½	17	28½	1¼
6	12½	32¼	32¼	11	27¾	38¾	8¼	25¼	42½	1¾
8	16	42¾	42¾	15	37	51¾	11	34	56¾	2½
10	21	53¾	53¾	18¾	46¼	65	13¾	42½	70¾	3
12	25	65	65	22¼	55½	77¾	16½	50¾	84¾	3¾

tion, tamp down and compact any loose soil, and build the footing forms on the soil. Either set the forms so that the top of the form will be the top of the footing, or use a level and carpenter's chalkline to mark the inside of the form at the elevation of the top of footing. Then place and secure any required reinforcing bars, and start the concrete pour.

The question of the size and spacing of reinforcing bars is too complicated to go into detail in this book, as entire thick technical volumes have been written on this solitary subject. Most concrete should contain at least minimal reinforcing, if only to resist cracking. We recommend that the advice of a competent engineer be obtained for all questions of reinforcing concrete and other structural matters. There are too many inherent variables in these matters to attempt to give off-the-cuff data here, as what would be just right for one home in certain dimensions and location, would be either overdone or inadequate under only slightly altered conditions. This is one area where the services of a professional are almost mandatory. The minor fee that may be charged for this advice will be well worth it in savings to you by avoiding either the expense of over-reinforcing or the hazard of deficient construction. This holds true in all other respects for your home, if you feel uncertain about any specific matter, doubt your own capability to either design or build a component, then hire a pro.

Once the size and spacing of reinforcing steel is determined, it is placed in the forms and secured. The spacing of bars will be set in three dimensions, and these bars have to be supported and rigidly braced so that the pouring of the concrete does not move them. Wire is most often used to tie together all bar joints and crossing points, and to suspend the bar mat at the correct height in the form. Rocks, bricks or blocks are also used to support reinforcing. If you use wood for temporary bracing, remember that it should be removed when enough concrete has been poured to hold the bars in place.

The concrete is poured into the forms without disturbing the reinforcing bar mat, and is layered throughout the length of the form. Pour each batch next to the previously deposited one, until the entire bottom of the form area is covered, and bring the level of the wet concrete gradually to the top of the form, keeping the mass fairly level throughout the pour. Place each batch into the form as near as possible to its final position, to avoid shoveling or flowing the concrete into place. As the concrete rises in layers, it must be consolidated by rodding or vibration. This aids the concrete density and prevents honeycombing, or pockets of air trapped in the mass. The rodding is done by repeatedly jabbing a bar, rod, shovel, etc., into the wet concrete until it has driven out all air pockets, and will harden in a smooth surface against the form. After the pour is completed, the excess concrete is struck off at the elevation of the footing top, and roughly finished with a length of scrap 2x4 drawn back and forth across the surface. Since it will not be exposed to view, the top of the footing will not need a smooth-troweled finish surface, but will require a keyway to tie the foundation wall to the footing. The keyway should lie along a line that is the center of both the footing and the foundation wall, as shown on the illustration below the foundation dimension table. A keyway is very simply made by placing a 2x4 onto the still-wet surface of the footing concrete along the centerline, forcing it down into the mass for the full thickness of the board, and leaving it there until the concrete sets up. All wood or form surfaces in contact with the poured concrete must be oiled to facilitate removal of the forms without damage to the concrete.

Concrete should be cured for at least seven days after the pour, and should not be permitted to dehydrate during that period. One curing method is to cover the mass with burlap as soon as it has taken its first set, that is, the surface has started to harden. The burlap is wet down, and kept wet for the full curing period. The forms should not be removed for at least 48 hours after completion of the pour. Care should be taken during the form removal to prevent damage to the fresh concrete, which must be recovered with the burlap and kept moist. The wet curing period is necessary to develop the full strength of the portland cement concrete, as if allowed to dry while setting, it can become brittle, and chip, flake and break easily.

The house floors and walls rest upon the foundation wall, which in turn rests upon the footing. The foundation wall is also best if built from portland cement concrete, for strength and convenient construction. Some excellent foundation walls have been built with bricks, concrete blocks, rubble stone, or other materials, but these all require hand placement of the individual components, taking a great deal more time and labor than a concrete foundation wall.

Make the kind of foundation wall you want, but we are only going to discuss concrete for this use. The width of the foundation wall depends upon the house wall thickness and the method and type of floor supports. The foundation wall will have to accommodate and support the floors of your home, thus the decision on this matter again must be made beforehand, so we return to our constant plea, plan, plan, and yet again, plan.

In current construction, most adobe homes are built with one of three different flooring methods; i.e., concrete slab on grade, that is, laid directly on ground surface; concrete slab above grade, with a crawl space under the house; and wood beam and girder above grade. Either of the latter two methods can be altered to accommodate basement construction, if you are determined to have one. The details of these three methods will be discussed in subsequent chapters, but all decisions must be made before you start construction, as if you change horses in midstream in these matters, you will surely get soaked.

In any case, the foundation wall must allow for the chosen flooring method, which generally means an extra three inch width from the footing up to the base of the flooring to provide a shelf or ledge to support the floor, or to tie it into the structure. The remaining width of the foundation wall should be at least an inch wider than the nominal house wall thickness. Thus, using a 24″ planned wall thickness for an example, the foundation wall would be 24″ plus 1″ plus 3″, or a total of 28″ nominal thickness or width. Remember that if you are concerned or dubious about proper dimensions, always go heavier rather than lighter. Your peace of mind is worth extra expenditures to dispel worry, when considering that you may live in this adobe home the rest of your days.

The construction forms for the foundation wall must be very substantially made, to hold straight, true lines and grades against the weight of the poured concrete. Don't try to skimp when building these forms, as quite literally the whole home will stand or fall upon them. Since the foundation wall will extend from the top of the footing to one foot above the ground-line, the wall may be from 6 to 8 feet high, depending upon your soil and ground surface. Do not use any lumber smaller than a standard 2x4 as framing on the forms, and don't be afraid to use lots of them. Build each form flat on the ground, then erect it in place, and brace it against the sides of the trench with great care. Place the inside form first, then whatever reinforcing steel you need or desire, then erect the outside form. For additional bracing and width control, you may add wood struts cut to the foundation wall width between the form faces, but please remember that these struts have to be removed as the poured concrete comes up to them. Use good half-inch or greater plywood to face the forms, and oil them well before erection, to prevent the hardened concrete from adhering to them when the time comes to remove them.

Treat the actual concrete pour as described for the footing, taking even greater care to rod and consolidate the mass to prevent voids and honeycombing. The foundation wall concrete pour must be done in one continuous operation, once started, it must be completed to avoid joints in the wall. Joints in a foundation wall must be avoided wherever it is humanly possible, as such joints lower the bearing strength of the wall, and create places where water may penetrate to cause rotting, erosion and possible subsidence of the home.

The top surface of the foundation wall must be smoothly finished to provide a flat surface upon which to erect the adobe walls. Remember that, if the foundation wall is not absolutely level, and properly squared in the designed location, the entire home may be twisted and warped. The ideal control for lines and grades for your adobe home is to have the basic line and elevation stakes set by a Surveyor or Engineer. If this is considered too expensive, you may lay out the site by batter-boards and stringlines.

Over the relatively short distances encountered in average home construction, a very tightly-drawn string may be considered to form a straight line, both horizontally and vertically. The conception of the batter-board arrangement is to provide a stable base from which tight stringlines may be stretched to form lines and grades from which offset measurements can be made. The batter-boards are set before any digging is done at the site. The location of the home upon the site is determined, and stakes or flagged nails are placed in the ground at the four major corners of the home. Then, offset measurements are made from these points to locate the outside corners of the batter-boards. Choose your own offset to fit your conditions, but keep it uniform throughout to avoid error-creating variations. The offset is required to put the lines back from the actual house wall line far enough so that the excavations and building operations may be done without destroying the batter-board layouts. This offset may be any distance from 5′ to 10′, so adopt an offset that fits your physical conditions. As with all other elements of your planning, record this data on paper, as a dimensioned sketch or table, and keep a permanent record.

Measure the offset distance, for instance ten feet, parallel to the planned house walls, and locate the cornerpoints of these offset lines, then drive a stake at each corner. These offset corner stakes shall be large and long enough to drive solidly in the ground, as the batter-boards will

depend upon the security of these points. The accuracy of location of these offset corner stakes is of paramount importance, as all major construction measurements will be referenced from them.

The 3:4:5 right triangle is helpful in laying out and checking these important control points. In this, a triangle whose sides are of 3 units, 4 units, and 5 units, always has a 90 degree right angle between the three and four unit sides. You can either make a large triangle of wood, or measure along sides, mark the 3 and 4 unit points, then measure a straight line along the hypotenuse of the triangle. If it comes out exactly 5, the enclosed angle is then 90 degrees. The offset corner stake which is at the highest point of natural ground should be driven to 12″ to 18″ above ground, and the other stakes are then driven to the same elevation. If you have access to a surveyor's level and rod, this is quickly done. If not, the leveling of the corners may be done the long, hard way, by trial and error with a carpenters' spirit level. The high corner stake is set to the desired height, and the other corner stakes are rough-set, and the internal angles are checked for accuracy, and stakes adjusted until all angles are correct. The other stakes are then driven until they appear to be barely higher than the control stake. Once you have set it, never touch or adjust that high corner control stake, but adjust all others to conform to it. To accomplish this, stretch a taut stringline along the outside of all the stakes, use a carpenter's spirit level to see how near level the strings are, then adjust the stakes by driving until all the lines are dead level. This takes two men to do with any speed, one to use the level, while the other drives the stakes. Do this slowly and carefully, and start out with the other stakes visibly higher than the control stake, as it's a good bit easier to drive a stake down an inch or two, than it is to pull it out, reset it, and get the top of it an inch higher.

After a long, tedious process of trial and error, inevitably mostly error, you have all the offset corner stakes secure, all enclosed right angles, and the tops of these stakes are all dead level in relation to each other. This level relationship is so important, that if you don't take the time and work to get them exactly level, why, you might as well not bother to put them up at all. To increase the speed and accuracy of checking the level, you may secure a 10' or longer, straight board to the carpenter's level, which gives a longer base to sight against the stringline, which must always be taut. This operation may take a seemingly unendurable time to resolve, but you have to do it right, so bear with it until done.

When the offset corner stakes are set, the rest of the batter-board assembly is erected. About 10' along each line from the corner stakes, drive stakes next to the stringline and level with the corners. Then, nail a board to both stakes, with the top level to both. The result will be solid wooden right angles parallel to the house walls and ten feet outside them. From these angles, you may stretch taut stringlines at any desired location, and measure directly from the stringlines for the desired construction point. These batter-board assemblies are to be left undisturbed in place until the actual adobe block-laying is under way, so that all measurements are from the same control base.

After the control network above has been established, the footing is located, formed, poured and cured; and the foundation wall has been located, formed, poured and finished at the design grade. The forms are stripped from the wall after 48 hours, the wet burlap, which was placed on the fresh concrete after the initial set, has been replaced on the wall, and is kept wet for at least seven days, and you are now ready to begin construction of the floors and walls of your adobe home.

This section has discussed foundation requirements in footing areas, concrete mixing and workmanship, foundation walls and line and grade control methods. We have set forth a few of the basic tenets and methods relating to these items, but only a few. As this book is by no means a definitive construction encyclopedia, all questions may perhaps not have been answered to your particular satisfaction, so, if you have need for further data, either study it yourself, or retain the services of a professional in that field. Please do not get the idea that merely by buying and studying this book, you have become a gold-plated authority on all phases of adobe home design and construction. The author is not that, so that you who read my words certainly cannot qualify either, on this basis alone.

A point that we have constantly belabored herein is that no one section of this book can stand alone. Each of the elements within are altered or affected by due consideration of other elements throughout the book. This is particularly true of this foundation section, which not only owes attention to soils, site, finance, etc., but also demands attention to plumbing, heating, electrical and other matters. The various utility facilities have to arrive into the home in some fashion, and certain of them will best be located under or through the footing or foundation wall.

Read the entire book, study the alternatives proposed herein, and make up your own mind, as it will be your adobe home, so it should be the way you want it, no one else. If you have serious doubts or questions on theory or your own ability in certain areas, hire a pro. If all this sounds familiar, it's because we have harped on the same theme throughout this book, so go to it and get it done, but get it done right.

CHAPTER VI

Floor Construction In Adobe Homes

Now that the foundation wall has been cast, the forms stripped, and the concrete cured, you are almost ready to begin, not laying block walls, but constructing the home floor. The floor, or subfloor should be done before the walls are erected. It's a good bit easier to build any type of subfloor with room to swing in, rather than cramped up inside exterior walls. After its construction, the subfloor will also afford clear, flat working area from which to erect the walls.

The subfloor has to integrate with the foundation wall, and your planning process will have decided upon the flooring type before the foundation wall was built. Which illustrates the full wheel of this particular vicious circle, in that adequate planning can lead to the answer to almost any problem. The basic decision you will have made in this case is which of the three or four flooring methods available that will be used in your adobe home. These methods include adobe floor on grade, concrete slab on grade, concrete slab with crawl space, or wood floor with crawl space. If necessary, either of the latter two types may be adapted to provide for basement construction.

However, before we get too involved with the vagaries of floor types, there is still work to do around the foundation walls. Do you remember all that soil that you painfully dug out of the ground to make room to build the footing and foundation wall? Well, now you will have the extremely doubtful pleasure of putting a great deal of that same soil right back into the

hole from which you dug it. When you completed the concrete work on the foundation wall, you left a large hole in the ground on both sides of it, clear down to the footing. This void must now be filled, and it must be thoroughly compacted as it is filled to preclude later subsidence. Don't run for the Webster's, as subsidence means sinking, which is what soil does when it is loosely dumped into a hole, and is in time compacted by weather and its own weight. The problem here is to prevent the subsidence, so the replaced soil must be compacted in layers as the hole is filled.

Unless you have access to construction equipment like pneumatic tampers, the soil will need to be pounded down into place by hand. A hand tamper can be bought or rented, or you can make your own from a piece of iron or steel plate and a broom-handle. Which leads us into another irrelevant thought; namely, don't throw away worn-out brooms, as those handles can be quite useful, even if you don't beat your wife. The heavy end of the tamper can be a flat plate of iron or steel about 6" square, and from 1/4 to 1/2" or so thick. Secure the plate to the end of the broomstick so that the bottom face of the plate is at right angles to the line of the broomstick, and there you have a tamper. The tamper should be heavy enough to work, but not so heavy that it will be too tiring to use for extended periods. So okay, the foundation wall concrete has been cured, you have a shovel and tamper at hand, and you are ready to begin backfilling the excavation.

Shovel loose soil into the hole all around the wall, on both sides, to a depth of 9″ to 10″ above the bottom, trying to keep the layer at least somewhat uniform. Then, get down in the bottom with your tamper, and start lifting and dropping, lifting and dropping, until you feel like dropping. Grasp the tamper handle with both hands, one above the other, and lift and drop, so that the flat face of the tamper pounds the soil into submission. The tamper must be moved slightly for each drop, so that the entire bottom of the trench receives equal time. There are all kinds of fancy tests to tell when the soil is adequately compacted, but the easiest test of all is that when the soil simply won't compact any more, it's dense enough. In many dry soils, you will have to add small quantities of water to aid the compactive effort, but do not overdo the water bit, as mud doesn't compact worth a darn. Each of these layers must be compacted on both sides of the wall before more soil is added, or you may cause unpleasant pressure differentials. Thus, layer by layer, the soil is pounded and pounded until you finally top out the hole. Sighs of blessed relief, perhaps too soon.

Because here is the zinger, here is the reason the bit on all this compaction and backfill is placed in the flooring section, rather than the foundation section. Some of the flooring types will demand that this same compaction be performed throughout the entire floor area of the home. Now, doesn't that bit of news make your blistered hands and aching back feel absolutely underwhelmed?

While performing this backfill, do not permit any trash, wood, leaves, organic soils, etc., to get into the compacted soil. These items will all rot, and eventually cause that old devil, subsidence. As we have said before, save all that organic soil for lawns and flowerbeds, don't waste it building unstable backfill. Thus, the backfill around the foundation wall is compacted in layers, right up to the level of the bottom of the lowest element in your chosen flooring system, which may mean that the complete floor area of the home must be compacted. As the foundation wall has already been constructed to accommodate the flooring system of your choice, we will at last proceed to discuss these choices.

One of the traditional floor types in adobe homes is, understandably, adobe itself. An adobe floor is built, not from blocks as are the walls, but from one solid mass of adobe. The entire floor area of the home must be leveled and compacted to a uniform grade at the elevation of the bottom of the adobe floor. The compaction of the subgrade below the floor must be very well done, as the adobe floor itself will also be compacted, and any soft spots in the subgrade will cause problems in obtaining a hard, even, level adobe floor. Opinions vary considerably on the optimum thickness for such floors, as the type of soil in the subgrade will have a significant effect on the stability of the soil floor. However, given adequate compaction on a decent subgrade, an adobe floor six inches thick should be enough for most homes.

The soil mixture for the adobe floor is blended to the same proportions of the adobe blocks, perhaps increasing the quantity of stabilizer by around 10%. When placing any floor system directly on grade; i.e., lying right down on the underlying ground or subgrade, a moisture barrier is needed between the interfaces. Polyethylene plastic sheeting has become the most convenient material for such moisture barriers. This plastic film comes in rolls of varying widths, and handles easily. After the subgrade has been compacted, the polyethylene is unrolled directly onto the prepared surface, with overlap between strips and bent up into all corners or vertical angles. When the entire subgrade has been sealed off with the plastic, begin placing the adobe mixture for the floor.

Place a layer of adobe over the whole floor area loosely, so that the polyethylene moisture barrier is protected from tearing or displacement. Compact this layer, again with your tamper and sweat, and place and compact the full floor thickness. This type of floor is hard to get level, and is of benefit mostly for traditionalists. It is quite true that most of the old adobe homes had adobe floors, but the main reason for such use was that no other material was available at rea-

TRADITIONAL ADOBE WALL CONSTRUCTION

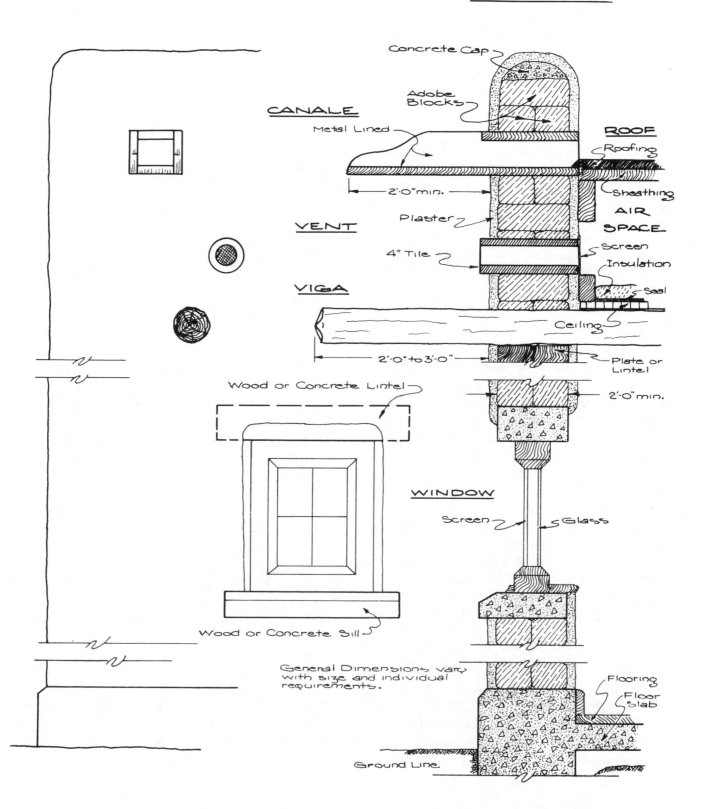

WALL SECTION

Concrete Cap

Adobe Blocks

CANALE

Metal Lined

2'-0" min.

VENT

Plaster

4" Tile

VIGA

2'-0" to 3'-0"

ROOF

Roofing

Sheathing

AIR SPACE

Screen

Insulation

Seal

Ceiling

Plate or Lintel

2'-0" min.

Wood or Concrete Lintel

WINDOW

Screen   Glass

Wood or Concrete Sill

Flooring

Floor Slab

General Dimensions vary with size and individual requirements.

Ground Line

sonable cost. An adobe floor can be durable and attractive, but we feel that its use may be limited to the adobe purist, as other floor systems are now available which are easier to build, are more amenable to vertical control and stability, and really don't cost an arm or leg.

You will note that throughout these discussions, we make a distinction between floors and flooring. For the purpose of this book, we shall refer to floors as the load-carrying elements of the system, the structural portion which supports the flooring and interior partitions. Flooring shall refer to the decorative or wearing surfaces above the floor, that is, the portion that you actually walk upon. This section shall, in general, discuss only the floors, while the flooring will be covered later in the interiors section. Some of the technical purists may scream at this aribtrary separation, but we feel that it may aid the understanding of some of these procedures by the layman, so we simply went ahead and did it.

In traditional usage, adobe constitutes both floor and flooring, as no decorative or wearing surface is placed upon it. A similar traditional floor system is that of brick. In the same fashion as adobe, ordinary fired building or paving brick form the structural and wearing surface of the floor system. Bricks make a very attractive floor, and are simple to maintain, but do require considerable effort to produce good results. Again, for any of the floor systems laid directly on grade, the entire surface of the soil underlying the complete home area will require leveling to grade and compaction. The bricks should not be laid upon the subgrade unless you have a fine sand in that strata. Most homes will require a sub-base of some sort between the existing soil and the bricks. Also, a polyethylene moisture barrier is to be laid just under the bricks, to seal off the entry or exit of moisture through the floor.

An excellent sub-base for brick floors is made with about four inches of sand or pea gravel laid into the area, leveled and smoothed. The moisture barrier is placed on top of this layer, and the bricks are then positioned in mortar on top.

The elevation control on this work will be critical, so as to produce a smooth, level floor. The spaces between the bricks are filled with mortar as they are laid, and the surface joints are then pointed. That is, the mortar between the bricks at the floor surface is struck off, and either finished smooth flush to the brick faces, or is given a slightly rounded finish below the face of the bricks. The surface of the completed floor should then be treated with one of the many sealers on the market. Sealers are now available in bases from varnish to plastic in much variety, so check out the products and select the one that fits your needs best. There are many who leave the brick floor unsealed, feeling that there is no need for it, but we think it should be done. In addition to sealing off moisture from the mortar and bricks, it also preserves color, is more sanitary, and eases cleaning. The brick floor takes a great deal of hard, precise labor, but it may be worth it to you for the end results.

Perhaps the most commonly-used floor system in the adobe home of today is the concrete slab poured directly on grade. With a bit of help, it is also the fastest and easiest of the systems. This system also requires the compaction of subgrade underlying the complete floor plan, so get your tamper out and sweat. Except for the top of the concrete slab, elevation control will not have to be so precise, although sloppy control will use up more concrete. When the subgrade is compacted, a four inch layer of pea gravel is placed and leveled, the polyethylene moisture barrier is laid, and the concrete is poured, and finished to the design grade.

Now, that sounds simple enough, so of course, it's not really that easy. Unless you use ready-mix concrete delivered to the site, the mixing of the concrete is a lot of work, and depositing it, vibrating and leveling, finishing, covering and curing are guaranteed to bring out some sweat. Mix the concrete as was set forth in the foundation section, and have your mixer set up as close to the house as you can get it, and still have room enough to work around it. The foundation wall will be your forms, and the finish top of that wall will be your slab elevation control. The

TYPICAL SECTION

ALTERNATE FRAMING
WOOD FLOOR

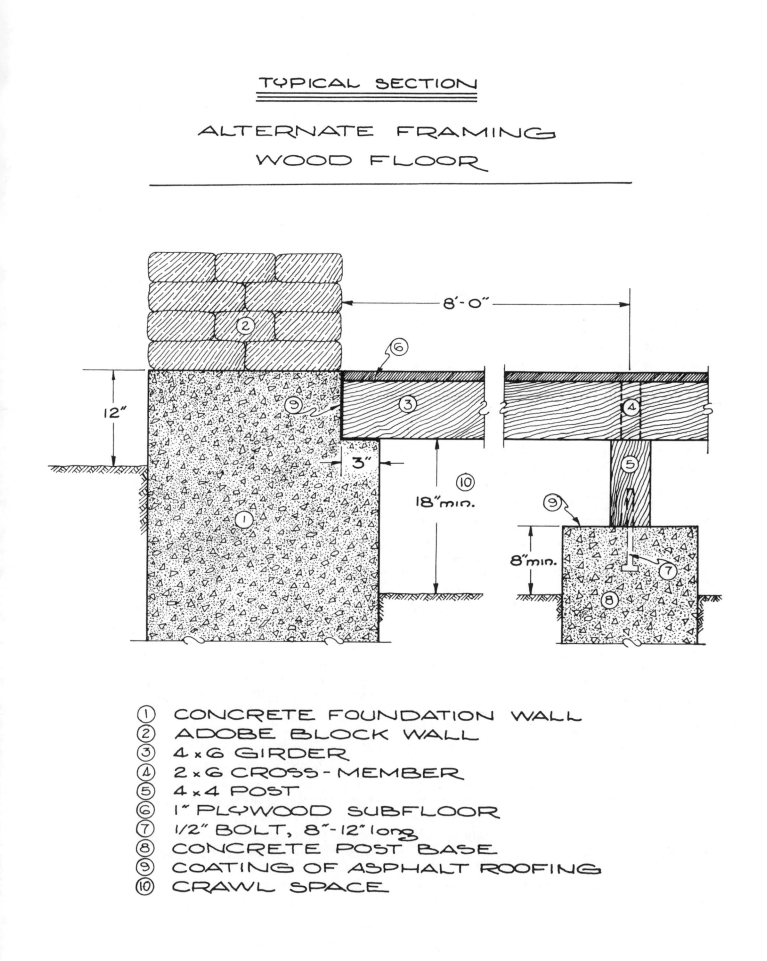

① CONCRETE FOUNDATION WALL
② ADOBE BLOCK WALL
③ 4 x 6 GIRDER
④ 2 x 6 CROSS-MEMBER
⑤ 4 x 4 POST
⑥ 1" PLYWOOD SUBFLOOR
⑦ 1/2" BOLT, 8"-12" long
⑧ CONCRETE POST BASE
⑨ COATING OF ASPHALT ROOFING
⑩ CRAWL SPACE

floor area may be too large for you to complete the pour in one operation. If so, you will have to divide the area into segments by building form dividers. Start the pour at the farthest point from your mixing operation, and work back towards it, so that you don't "paint yourself into a corner." You simply cannot push a wheelbarrow full of concrete over a mass of wet, fresh concrete, so don't try. Fill the barrow at the mixer, push it over wide boards you will have already laid down as runners to the farthest point of the floor, and pour each batch onto the floor as close to its final location as possible. Don't try to move the concrete mass around much, as this leads to segregation, which is not good whether it's people or concrete. To finish each segment, you will need a board longer than the width of the segment, which is rested on both sides of the forms or walls, then dragged back and forth across the surface to strike off the excess concrete. Long-handled wood floats and bars are then used to give a smooth, even finish to the concrete floor. This operation is critical to give good results, and unless you have finished concrete slabs before, you had better find a friend who has, as you don't become a mason overnight.

The top surface of the concrete slab must be level and smooth, without any dips or hollows, or other severe irregularities, as the final flooring will be placed directly upon this slab, and will reflect all of the errors and defects of the slab surface. As soon as the concrete has taken its initial set, that is, the concrete has hardened to the touch, it must be protected to start the week-long curing period. Wet burlap or straw laid over the slab and kept continuously moist is one traditional method of curing. There are now spray membrane compounds on the market which do almost as well. A major consideration in curing concrete is to retard moisture loss while the concrete is reaching set strength. Without proper curing, the concrete will never reach its design strength, and will be subject to severe cracking and spalling.

These direct on grade floor systems vary primarily in the material used, and all have the same benefits and liabilities. The prime benefit is that they are faster and cheaper to build than the above-grade types. A major liability is that all pipes and ductwork for heating, plumbing, or electrical facilities are either buried under, or embedded in the floor. Thus, the quality control on materials and construction for these facilities is critical, as they are simply unavailable for repair without tearing up the floor. There we go again, you just cannot resolve any one decision regarding your home construction without giving full consideration to three or four other problems. The only answer is to plan, plan, and yet again, plan.

The above-grade floor systems also vary in the materials used, whether concrete slab and beam, or wood beam and girder, or even the relatively rare use in housing of steel girder-type construction. The design of an above-grade floor system is much more critical than the on-grade types, as the floor and interior wall loadings will be concentrated at the support points, and will require individual design for each home. Several drawings are set forth herein to illustrate these floor system types, but we recommend that advice of a competent professional be obtained for detailed design.

Several of the advantages of the above-grade floor systems include some degree of accessibility to piping, ductwork, and conduits, and also the opportunity to provide a basement or cellar. However, the problems of greater complexity, probable longer construction time, and increased cost must be evaluated. You may also have already noted that all of the floor plans included in this book are for single-story construction. Multiple-story adobe homes are not only possible, but practical. However, the complexities inherent in the structural, wiring, piping, plumbing and heating aspects of multi-story construction would make this book even bigger, thicker, wordier, and more expensive than it is already. The intent of this work is to provide average answers to the problems of adobe home construction for the average home. We could not possibly include detail design data for all possible permutations, and so have deliberately limited the work to resolution of average needs.

Complex structures in adobe are feasible, but must be individually designed by a professional. If you want such a home, and can afford it, retain an architect or engineer, and more power to you.

For the average needs, again study the alternatives offered here, consider the benefits and liabilities, and make up your own mind what you want and can afford.

CHAPTER VII

Adobe Walls

After endless dissertation and recrimination, we eventually arrive at the heart of the adobe home, the one thing that makes it unique among housing types, its adobe block walls. Various "authorities" have conducted alleged "studies" of the asserted benefits to be derived from adobe wall construction. Even several of the giant utility firms got into the act, setting forth their own versions of heat-loss or insulation needs tables, mostly to attempt to push their own services. A great many of these so-called studies were either purely limited theory, or were based upon inadequate data, erroneous conclusions, or just plain old bias or prejudice.

It is an indisputable fact that earth walls per inch of thickness do not have the insulating quality of such insulating materials as pumice, sawdust, polyurethane, or other materials of equal thickness. And therein lies the rub, "per inch of equal thickness." Probably no one with much sense would deny that an adobe wall six inches thick is vastly inferior in insulative quality to conventional insulated wood-frame construction or insulated cinder block walls. But, this argument is absurd on its face, as a six inch adobe wall not only does not insulate, it might not even stand up alone. The person that builds a thin adobe wall is simply wasting his time, and may just as well build frame or cinder block, then glob it up with stucco to imitate adobe.

Aside from aesthetics, which cannot be ignored, a major benefit of adobe walls derives from the sheer mass of the thick earth walls. An adobe wall less than two feet thick is just not good adobe. Examine any of the historic adobe buildings around the world, which have survived the crucial test of five, six, or more centuries of useful life. One look at the massive thickness of those walls will prove that those old folks knew what they were doing. For what counts in an adobe home is not what theory says will result from comparative efficiencies per inch of thickness, but what actually does happen. Thick adobe walls do produce an excellent insulative effect as the result of a phenomenon known to science as the "thermal flywheel" effect. We will make no attempt to explain this phenomenon, but what happens is that the sheer bulk mass of the wall absorbs heat during sunlight radiation periods, and then slowly releases this stored heat during the colder nocturnal hours. The result is that the temperature inside the home remains remarkably constant without artificial assistance. The various studies that have attacked adobe qualities attempt to compare equal thickness walls of differing construction methods, which is about as sensible as comparing the effects of drinking a quart each of milk or tequila. It should be obvious that all materials have optimum uses, including the quantity or thickness particularly suited to use or consumption which is ideal for that item. But, just try telling that to some of our current egghead theorists.

A particular benefit of adobe is its adaptability to the needs and purse of the do-it-yourself folks. An adobe home, built to your own design with two-foot-thick walls by a contractor, will certainly cost more money than either conven-

tional frame or cinder-block construction. What the pundits tend to ignore is that such a home is also worth more money on the open housing market. However, an adobe home can be built with your own hands, and perhaps those of your friends, at a much lower total dollar outlay than could almost any other type of house with an equal floor area. If you roll your own adobe blocks, the purchase of construction materials will be at significantly lower dollar cost than other types, which will require that you purchase concrete blocks, lumber, siding, sheathing, insulation, and on and on, for which items you have substituted adobe blocks. Thus, for a given amount of money, plus a generous allotment of sweat and backache, it is possible to obtain a lot more house by building your own adobe. For the non-existent average man, it may be the only way that he will ever get a custom-built home, tailored to his own particular needs and desires, rather than some jimcrack mass-produced development junk.

The aesthetics of an adobe home are undeniable, but only if they suit the personal taste of the persons involved. We have all met the easterner who is aghast at the thought of living in a "dirty old mud house." Which only shows that ignorance produces prejudice in most circumstances, while familiarity and knowledge lead to tolerance, acceptance, and even admiration. We continue to digress, especially since those who do not want adobe homes will not check this book out of the library, much less purchase a copy. Since the whole premise of this book is the construction of adobe block homes, we have to support our own conclusions, as we would dearly love to sell at least a few copies of the blasted thing.

We now presume that the home has been designed, the adobe blocks manufactured, footing and foundation wall cast, cured and backfilled, and the basic floor system has been installed, and you are now ready to start upon the walls of your home. Well, perhaps not quite. . . .

Before the block-laying starts, the location of all wall openings is to be measured off and marked on the foundation wall, and mortar is mixed. The wall openings will include doors,

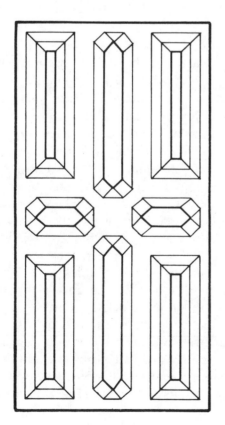

DOORS FOR ADOBE HOMES

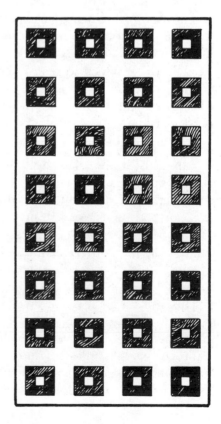

windows, ventilators, perhaps utility facilities, and even canales and vigas. One method to keep track of all these openings is to make yourself a checklist of all wall openings, and mark them against the block course level in which the bottom of the opening occurs. As always, it is much better to spend the time and effort to plan ahead, than to lose time and money breaking holes through two feet of wall to accommodate a forgotten item. There is a difference of opinion among the experts on when the frames should be inserted in the opening. Some few feel that the window and door frames should be left out of the wall until the block-laying is completed, and state the settlement of the blocks should occur before the frames are installed. Rather more experts feel that frames should be inserted as the wall is built, so that the blocks will be laid directly against the frames. Suit yourself, but we feel that door frames should be erected before blocks are laid, and that window and other opening frames must be inserted as the block wall reaches the level of the bottom of the frame.

The mortar is mixed to the same proportions as the adobe blocks, as a difference in strength in the items can lead to some shrinkage or cracking problems. The only change in the two mixes should be that the adobe soil may need to be put through a fine screen to remove or break up all the larger particles. This is done only to avoid the presence of larger particles which may be troublesome while adjusting blocks and spreading or pointing the mortar.

Perhaps this is the place to insert a short dissertation on doors and windows. Due to the extreme diversity of styles and sizes that are now available for both units, we will make no recommendations whatsoever as to sizes, styles or conformation. The one fairly recent development in these facilities which we shall urge you to use is the completely pre-assembled window and door units. This saves a good bit of labor in building frames, setting and pointing glass, and hanging and adjusting doors. These are all fairly ticklish items for the neophyte to attempt, and could result in some broken glass and uneven doors. The pre-assembled units are so complete that

they need only to be slipped into a prepared opening, then screwed into the 2x4 framing which was put in while the block wall was being erected. This also indicates the demand for adequate planning, as the window and door units must be chosen before the block-laying is performed, so that the 2x4 framing may be inserted sized so that the pre-assembled units fit exactly inside the framing. Also, all window units should have thermopane glass, to aid in lowering heat loss.

After the door frames have been located, placed and securely braced in position, the block-laying may commence. However, before any mortar is mixed, the complete bottom course of adobe blocks is laid around the perimeter of the home. The blocks are laid loosely, without mortar, at what is assumed to be proper spacing; i.e., approximately one-quarter inch apart. The benefit of this seemingly wasteful operation is that each block may be adjusted in spacing as required, to avoid the use of too many half or quarter blocks in each course. After the blocks have been adjusted to obtain maximum benefit from varied spacing, the bottom course may be mortared, and the spacing repeated in higher courses.

Each successive layer of blocks must be coursed, or placed in the wall overlapping the joint between blocks in the lower course, so as not to develop a continuing vertical joint. In addition, the longitudinal or transverse laying of blocks should be alternated in series, so as to tie the full thickness of the wall together. We have advocated a minimum wall thickness of two feet, and, for convenience in handling, an adobe block nominally 12"x8"x4" in size. With these dimensions, when the block is placed longitudinally; i.e., with the length of the block in line with the face of the wall, three parallel blocks are needed to make up the wall thickness. When the alternate block is placed transversely; i.e., with the length of the block at right angles to the face of the wall, two end-to-end blocks provide the full wall thickness. This coursing aids in controlling cracking, stabilizes the full wall thickness, and promotes wall strength by eliminating continuous vertical joints. Each successive

"COURSING" AN ADOBE WALL

NOTE HOW ALTERNATE LAYERS OR "COURSES" ARE STAGGERED TO AVOID VERTICAL JOINTS.

This Example illustrates a 24" thick Adobe Wall built with 11⅞" x 7⅞" x 3⅞" Adobe Blocks. (Nominal 12"x8"x4")

Adobe Blocks of this size may weigh from 20 to 30 pounds each, depending on density of the materials.

layer in height must be controlled both vertically and horizontally, so that the wall is built both level and straight.

One method to aid in this control is the taut stringline. Straight boards or stakes are erected at each end of the wall, with one face of each stake in line with the desired line of the wall. A stringline is then tautly stretched between the stakes, at the measured elevation of the next block course to be laid. With the aid of small blocks under the string, the stringline is offset outward a definite distance, such as one inch, from the desired line of the wall face. Both vertical and horizontal control are thus established, as each outside block is laid so that its top face is in the same plane as the taut stringline, and its outside face is parallel to, and one inch inside, that line. As each course is completed, the stringline is moved upward the measured distance to the top of the next course. Do not erect the full height of a single wall by itself, but attempt to keep the entire wall perimeter of the home near the same course level.

When the laid block courses reach the level of the bottom of the window unit, the concrete or wooden sill, the sill and window frame are located, erected and braced, and the wall coursing is continued until the top of the window frame is reached. The concrete lintel is then laid in place over the window or door frame, to spread the load of the wall over the opening to the wall adjacent to the opening. The blocks are then laid to the top of the wall, when the perimeter beam or roof lintel is laid along the top of the wall to support the roof construction. This brief explanation ignores the sweat and backache that will occur during all this labor. Speaking of backache, the most efficient and painless blocklaying is accomplished at or near waist level. As the completed height of the wall rises, the worker must obviously also rise.

Scaffolding will be required to elevate the worker to efficient heights to perform the labor. These scaffolds, although temporary in nature, must be strong, secure, and safe, with emphasis on the safe. One of the old bromides of the

construction joke-book concerns the mason who was laying brick facing from a scaffold at the fifteenth floor level of a new building, who stepped back to admire his work. They buried him between two mortarboards. We didn't include that morbid joke to be funny, but to illustrate the fact that you can get seriously hurt while building your own home, if you don't follow all the basic safety precautions. Scaffolding must be safe, and if you don't quite feel up to building it, then almost anything may be obtained from rental firms nowadays. Metal pipe is increasingly being used as a framework for scaffolding, although wood is still in use. For your own sake, and that of your dependents, don't sling a 2x12 between two stepladders, and expect to survive working from it.

The mortar is mixed to the same proportions, and with the same methods, as the adobe blocks. Use the portable concrete mixer again to save time and labor. The placing of the mortar is simple, and you will get plenty of practice at it to attain full mastery of the craft. Several hand tools will be needed, as a hammer, a level, and both large and small trowels. The placing of the mortar may be accomplished with some varying techniques, all of which attain the same ends by very slightly differing means. Therefore, the technique chosen really doesn't matter, except that it should suit your own preferences. One method that particularly suits us, is to lay mortar with two swipes of the large trowel onto the surface upon which the block is to be laid. The two swipes of that trowel will leave beads of mortar along both edges of the underlying block, which, when the block being laid is slapped into place, will become squeezed into one adequate thin layer of mortar. Also, the face of the new block which will be placed against the face of a block already laid, will be "buttered" with another swipe of the trowel, leaving a blob of mortar that will be flattened to a thin layer when the block is slammed into position. This is not as complicated as this somewhat labored explanation may seem, as you may be pleasantly surprised at how quickly you grow to master this work.

REINFORCED CONCRETE LINTELS

SECTION

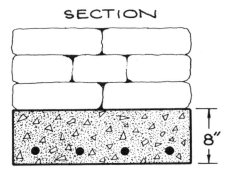

8"

PLAN

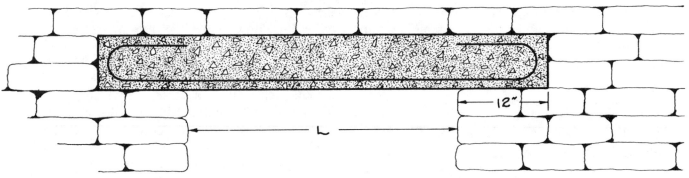

L   12"

REINFORCING BARS

L CLEAR OPENING	WALL THICK.	REINF. BARS
3'	12"	2 - ¼" ∅
	16"	3 - ¼" ∅
	24"	4 - ¼" ∅
4'	12"	2 - 3/8" ∅
	16"	3 - 3/8" ∅
	24"	4 - 3/8" ∅
6'	12"	2 - ½" ∅
	16"	3 - ½" ∅
	24"	4 - ½" ∅
8'	12"	2 - 5/8" ∅
	16"	3 - 5/8" ∅
	24"	4 - 5/8" ∅

The Length of each Bar shall be 3'-6" plus "L".

The Length of each Lintel shall be 2'-0" plus "L".

NOTES

LINTELS ARE REQUIRED OVER ALL WALL OPENINGS

THE LINTEL SHALL BE THE FULL THICKNESS OF THE ADOBE WALL, & MAY BE COVERED WITH PLASTER, WOOD TRIM, ETC.

THE CLEAR OPENING, "L", IS MEASURED FROM WALL FACE TO WALL FACE, NOT TO THE LESSER FRAMED OPENING.

LINTELS ARE PRECAST, CURED, & STOCKPILED. CAST SEVERAL EXTRAS TO ALLOW FOR SOME BREAKAGE OR REVISIONS.

PLACE REINFORCING BARS TO PERMIT ONE FULL INCH CLEARANCE FROM FORMS.

WHEN FINISHING CONCRETE, MARK THE TOPS OF LINTELS TO PREVENT UPSIDE- DOWN INSTALLING.

If the outside adobe wall is to be plastered, fine trimming or beading of the mortar joints is not desirable. A slight gap between the mortar and the face of the block will aid plastering, by giving a tiny slot for the plaster to grip. If the wall is to be left unplastered, either bare, whitewashed or painted, all of the mortar joints must be pointed. Again, there are several finishes to evaluate. One method is to fill the joint completely with mortar, then smooth it off flush to the face of the brick. An alternative is to fill the joint not quite full, and then smooth it inward with a small trowel or pointer, so that the surface of the mortar forms an arc or angle pointing into the wall. The level is used frequently to check the block placement. It is laid both along the line of the wall, and also transversely across the thickness of the wall. Tilted blocks will ruin a wall, no matter which way the tilt slopes. The vertical alignment of the wall is spot-checked with a plumb bob, which you don't have to buy, as it is a snap to make. Just a small, heavy weight, such as a very large lead sinker, which is secured to the end of a long, light cord or string. With the weight hanging free above ground, under other than gale conditions, the string will form a vertical line. Suspend the plumb bob so that the string is a measured distance from any point on the wall, and all points in the same vertical plane as the string should be the same distance from it as the check point. If not, you have a sloping wall, and had darn well better correct it.

Another decision to be made is whether or not to plaster the exterior of your adobe home. There is a slight tendency in a few regional areas to leave the outside wall unplastered, perhaps bare, whitewashed or painted. This produces an aspect which is pleasing to some, but on this point we completely agree with the traditionalists, in that an unplastered adobe wall really isn't right for an adobe home. With the utilization of adequate stabilizers, a plastered exterior wall is not demanded for protection from moisture, and thus becomes a matter of personal preference in aesthetics. So leave the outside walls unplastered if that is your wish, but bear with us while we discuss plastering with adobe for those other folks.

We have continually harped upon the benefits of homogeneity in the adobe home, so, quite naturally, the advocated plaster mixture is yet again the same as the mortar and adobe blocks. The soil is also run through a fine-mesh screen to break down or remove the larger bits, only to avoid clots or clods in the plaster, which may be troublesome to work onto the wall face. The stabilizer content of the mix may be increased slightly, and color can be acquired through the natural shade of the adobe mix, the blending of powdered pigment into the plaster, or through conventional painting over the face of the plaster coat. The plaster may need some assistance to adhere well to the wall face, for which purpose, the traditional solution has been the suspension of wire mesh, such as chicken-wire fencing, down and a bit away from the face of the block wall. The mesh must be held away from the face of the blocks to provide a grip for the plaster. If the mesh is allowed to dangle loosely down the wall, the act of plastering will force the mesh right against the block face, so it may as well not be there. To hold the mesh out the required distance, it must be secured to the wall about every other row of blocks with either plasterer's or double-headed nails.

The actual techniques of applying the plaster are not difficult, but do require practice to become truly adept. If your project should include an adobe garden wall, or some other decorative adobe wall that is not part of the house, that wall can be the first plastered, so that the techniques have been mastered before the home is attempted. Past practice in adobe plastering has been to wait up to several months after the walls were completed to do the plastering. This period of time was then needed to allow the unstabilized adobe blocks to cure and settle under the weight loading of the wall. However, if your blocks have been adequately stabilized, the blocks cured before the walls are erected, the normal time lag of a do-it-yourselfer should provide all the time needed between erection and plastering.

Don't be too concerned if your plastering efforts do not produce a mirror smooth wall surface, as that isn't the adobe criteria. The nature of the blocks and the mortar preclude such finishes, and are not intended for adobe homes. There is a distinctive charm to the finish of adobe mortar that blends beautifully into the aesthetic effect of the total home, somewhat roughhewn, a touch uneven, yet withal merging the whole into an aspect gladdening the heart of any adobe aficionado.

Now that the exterior walls of your adobe home have been completed, your thoughts may turn to the roofing of the structure. However, it is not quite yet time, as unless your home is quite narrow, at least several of the interior walls must be erected to bear the load of the other end of the vigas or roof joists. In most homes, at least one load-bearing interior wall is included, which may extend roughly down the middle for the full length of the home. The length of clear span; i.e., the distance between the point of roof support over the outside wall and the point of support over the inside load-bearing wall, depends upon the materials used for the structural members of the roof. This comment runs right back to our constant plea for detailed planning, as the clear span capability of the roof members will dictate the location of load-bearing walls, and thus must be considered at the time that the floor plan of your adobe home is first being contemplated.

We will assume that you have made your own determinations of clear spans, based somewhat upon our further comments on roof support elements and interior layout and planning, and proceed to discuss the construction of the load-bearing interior walls. For such walls, you have a basic choice between conventional wood-framed or adobe walls. Either type has its separate attractions, and will afford benefits and liabilities that must be evaluated in accordance to your own particular needs and desires. It's your home, and the decisions on basic alternatives are all yours. We shall set forth the differing bits and pieces while offering our comments, and although some of our personal prejudices may shine through these comments like a beacon, it is still up to you.

Interior walls of the same adobe block as the exterior walls offer certain advantages in aesthetics, homogeneity, and less direct cost for purchased construction materials. The materials, methods and construction of an inside adobe wall may be exactly the same as that of the outside walls, perhaps with the single exception of the finishing or plastering. Lintels will again be required over all door openings, and a roof lintel or beam must be placed along the top of the wall to support the roof members. An inside adobe wall should be built at the same time as the outside walls, so that the blocks may be intertied with the coursing of the outside wall to develop strength and stabilize the corners. It is our personal feeling that interior adobe walls should not be plastered, only whitewashed or painted. The aesthetic effect of the then-visible adobe block pattern is similar to that of some stone or brick interior walls, which is beautiful to some and abhorent to others. We feel that there are almost unlimited decorator possibilities inherent to the combinations of painted adobe blocks with the diversity of paneling, painting or papering of conventional wood-frame interior walls. To us, a fireplace should always be located against a painted or whitewashed adobe wall, both for aesthetics and convenience in construction.

The possible disadvantages of interior adobe walls include the construction time and labor, the placement of utility pipes, wiring and ductwork, and the floor space taken up by the thickness of an adobe wall. However, these comparatively minor disadvantages also apply to exterior walls, and you must like adobe or you wouldn't be this far into this book, so have at it. The thickness of walls is a point that must be kept in mind throughout your planning. The floor space of a room is from face to face of the walls, and the wall thickness, whether the approximate six inches of conventional wood-framing or the several feet of adobe, must be included in the dimensional layouts to avoid winding up with odd-sized rooms or too-narrow halls, entries, or

INTERIOR WALLS

Produces an average interior wall 5½" to 6" thick.

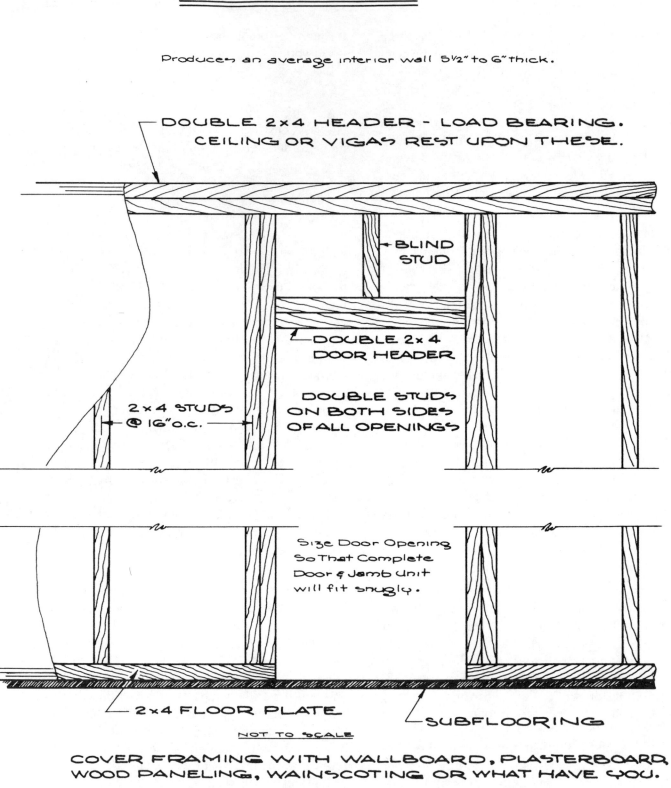

**DOUBLE 2x4 HEADER - LOAD BEARING.
CEILING OR VIGAS REST UPON THESE.**

→BLIND
STUD

**DOUBLE 2x4
DOOR HEADER**

**DOUBLE STUDS
ON BOTH SIDES
OF ALL OPENINGS**

**2x4 STUDS
@ 16" o.c.**

Size Door Opening
So That Complete
Door & Jamb Unit
will fit snugly.

2x4 FLOOR PLATE

SUBFLOORING

NOT TO SCALE

COVER FRAMING WITH WALLBOARD, PLASTERBOARD,
WOOD PANELING, WAINSCOTING OR WHAT HAVE YOU.
OR
IGNORE THIS PAGE, AND USE SINGLE-BLOCK
THICKNESS ADOBE FOR ALL INTERIOR WALLS.

other clearances. All load-bearing adobe walls inside the home should be the same thickness as the exterior walls, so as to equalize the loading from the roof and prevent unequal settlement. This could lead to tilted ceilings, cracking or failing of a too-thin adobe load-bearing wall. Non-load-bearing adobe walls, those that act only as partitions between rooms, may be built of single-thickness of blocks to save time, labor and floor space.

Conventional wood-frame interior walls take less time and labor than adobe to erect, but also require greater cash outlay to purchase the construction materials. They are also easier to alter at some future date, for possible floor plan revisions or redecorating. These walls can be built flat upon the floor, then tilted to the vertical and set solidly into place. This somewhat eases and simplifies the work of constructing these units.

The base of the wood-frame wall is the 2x4 floor plate, which supports or secures all other elements. This board is laid accurately along the desired line of the wall, then secured rigidly to the sub-floor. If you have chosen one of the concrete floor alternates, this fastening could give some problems. A solution to this is cartridge power-driven studs. A cartridge-powered stud driver may be rented or purchased, and can be indispensable for attaching wood permanently to either concrete or adobe. The vertical 2x4 studs are located at each end of the wall, and on 16″ centers throughout its length. The position of each door or other wall opening is determined, and double 2x4 studs are placed at 16″ centers vertically between the door header and the roof header or top plate, which may also be doubled 2x4s.

The roof header, which is secured to all of the vertical studs, may also be of either doubled 2x6 or 2x8 if extra strength or width is needed. Diagonal 2x4 bracing is generally also provided at all corners or door openings. The floor plate is omitted through the width of door openings, and the double wall studs are set an exact distance apart, so that the selected door frame and jamb unit will be a snug fit within. The studs and headers or plates are usually toe-nailed; i.e., a nail is driven diagonally through the stud near its end, so as to penetrate the other board and secure it rigidly. Toe-nailing can be enervating for the novice, so that if you are as bad at it as we are, we recommend the use of a sheet metal device known as metal joist stirrups, metal grips, and a great many trade names. This device is a thin square of sheet metal, perhaps 4″ x 4″, with slots or cuts at intervals along all sides, and holes spaced uniformly on the surface. This item may be bent so as to surround and support the juncture of two boards, and nails are driven through the holes at right angles to the surface. This both avoids improperly done toe-nailing, and strengthens the joint.

The roof header, or top plate, is the item upon which the vigas, roof beams, girders or joists rest in load-bearing walls. Doubled top plates must be used for strength in load-bearing walls, while non-load bearing walls, acting only as partitions, may be built with single top plates. When cutting your wall studs, remember which type the stud is going into, as the difference between single and double top plates will make a difference to the required length of the stud. Unless you have some particular need or desire for greater clearances, make the floor to ceiling height eight feet, as most wallboards, plasterboards or paneling are made in 4′ x 8′ stock sizes. This affords the greatest degree of use without waste, splicing, odd bits or custom sizing.

The lumber purchased for studs, headers, joists or plates should be Number Two Common or better for any wood that will be a permanent structural, but invisible, element of the home construction. We have supplied several pages of tables, illustrations and other data on nails, lumber and suchlike, and have probably glossed over some of the difficulties that may be encountered in the construction of your adobe home. However, it is felt that there is too much data required to delineate the adobe home, without attempting to make you a master carpenter in the process.

BASIC LUMBER DIMENSIONS

NOMINAL SIZE	ACTUAL SIZE	BOARD FEET PER FOOT	TYPICAL USE
1" x 2"	25/32" x 1 5/8"	0.17	SHEATHING FURRING & TRIM
1" x 3"	25/32" x 2 5/8"	0.25	
1" x 4"	25/32" x 3 5/8"	0.34	
1" x 5"	25/32" x 4 5/8"	0.42	
1" x 6"	25/32" x 5 5/8"	0.50	
1" x 8"	25/32" x 7 1/2"	0.67	
1" x 10"	25/32" x 9 1/2"	0.84	
1" x 12"	25/32" x 11 1/2"	1.00	
2" x 2"	1 5/8" x 1 5/8"	0.33	STRUCTURAL, FRAMING & OTHER HEAVY
2" x 3"	1 5/8" x 2 5/8"	0.50	
2" x 4"	1 5/8" x 3 5/8"	0.67	
2" x 6"	1 5/8" x 5 5/8"	1.00	
2" x 8"	1 5/8" x 7 1/2"	1.33	
2" x 10"	1 5/8" x 9 1/2"	1.67	
2" x 12"	1 5/8" x 11 1/2"	2.00	

BASIC LUMBER GRADES

GRADE	STANDARD	TYPICAL USE
SELECT	GOOD APPEARANCE, NATURAL FINISHING QUALITIES.	ALL FINISH WORK
A	BEST QUALITY CLEAR WOOD	FINE CABINETWORK, INTERIORS, TRIM
B	FEW SLIGHT IMPERFECTIONS	CABINETWORK, TRIM, PANELING, FLOORING
C	SMALL DEFECTS & BLEMISHES	HIGH QUALITY PAINT FINISH
D	SMOOTH SURFACE	MILLWORK, MOLDINGS, BUILT-INS, FIXTURES
COMMON	CONSTRUCTION & UTILITY NOT FOR FINISH WORK	HEAVY OR TEMPORARY WORK
1	HAS KNOTS, BUT SOUND & TIGHT. LIMITED DEFECTS	GENERAL PURPOSE, SIDING, SHELVING, PANELING
2	TIGHT-GRAINED, LARGE & COARSE DEFECTS.	FORMWORK, SHEATHING, SUBFLOORS
3	ROUGH, KNOT HOLES	TEMPORARY WORK
4	VERY LOW QUALITY	CHEAP-GRADE WORK
5	POOREST STANDARD GRADE	VERY ROUGH WORK, BOXES, CRATES.

WOODWORKING JOINTS

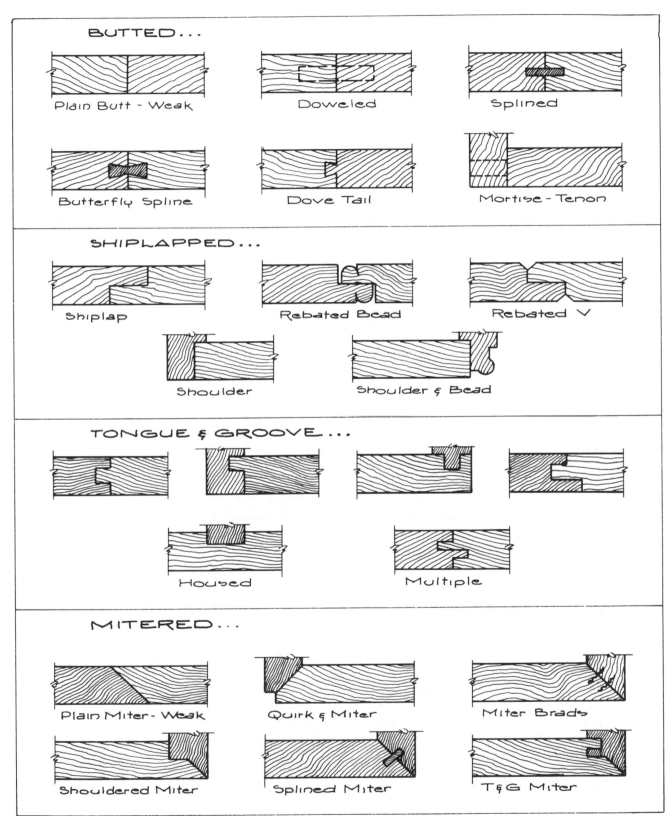

BUTTED...

Plain Butt - Weak

Doweled

Splined

Butterfly Spline

Dove Tail

Mortise - Tenon

SHIPLAPPED...

Shiplap

Rebated Bead

Rebated V

Shoulder

Shoulder & Bead

TONGUE & GROOVE...

Housed

Multiple

MITERED...

Plain Miter - Weak

Quirk & Miter

Miter Brads

Shouldered Miter

Splined Miter

T & G Miter

PLYWOOD STOCK TYPES

ALL AVAILABLE IN 4' x 8' SHEETS

GRADE	FACE	BACK	THICKNESSES	TYPICAL USE
EXT-DFPA : EXTERIOR TYPE				
A - A	A	A	1/4, 3/8, 1/2, 5/8, 3/4	OUTDOOR FURNITURE, FENCES, MARINE
A - B	A	B	1/4, 3/8, 1/2, 5/8, 3/4	AS ABOVE, WHERE ONE SIDE IS LESS IMPORTANT
PLYSHIELD	A	C	1/4, 3/8, 1/2, 5/8, 3/4	SIDING, GABLE ENDS, SOFFITS, BREEZEWAYS
UTILITY	B	C	1/4, 3/8, 1/2, 5/8, 3/4	UTILITY OUTDOOR PANELS
SHEATHING	C	C	3/8, 1/2, 5/8	ROUGH CONSTRUCTION
PLYFORM	B	B	3/4	CONCRETE FORMS
INTERIOR TYPE				
INT. A-A	A	A	1/4, 3/8, 1/2, 5/8, 3/4	FURNITURE, CABINETWORK, BUILT-INS, PARTITIONS
INT. A-B	A	B	1/4, 3/8, 1/2, 5/8, 3/4	AS ABOVE, ONE SIDE LESS IMPORTANT
PLYPANEL	A	D	1/4, 3/8, 1/2, 5/8, 3/4	WALL PANELING, ETC.
PLYBASE	B	D	1/4, 3/8, 1/2, 5/8, 3/4	BASE & BACKING MAT'L.
PLYSCORD	C	D	3/8, 5/16, 1/2, 5/8	SHEATHING, SUBFLOORS
PLYFORM	B	B	5/8, 3/4	SMOOTH CONC. FORMS

TYPICAL HARDBOARDS

USE	THICKNESS (IN.) SOLID BACKING				THICKNESS (IN.) OPEN BACKING				TYPE
	1/8	3/16	1/4	5/16	1/8	3/16	1/4	5/16	
DOORS	●				●	●	●		C, E, G
DRAWERS					●	●	●		B, C, F, G
FLOORS		●	●						C
EXT. CEILING		●	●		●	●	●		A, C
EXT. WALLS		●	●	●		●	●		C
INT. CEILING	●	●				●	●		A, B, C
INT. WALLS	●	●				●	●		A, B, C, D, E
WAINSCOTS	●	●				●	●		C, D, E
DIVIDERS					●	●			F, G
CASE-BACKS	●	●			●	●	●		A, B, C, D, E, F, G
CASE-ENDS	●	●			●	●			A, B, C, D, E, F, G
COUNTER TOPS	●	●					●	●	C, E

HARDBOARD TYPES

A - Panelwood
B - Std. Presdwood
C - Tempered Presdwood
D - Temprtile
E - Leatherwood
F - Std. Duolux
G - Tempered Duolux

NAILS

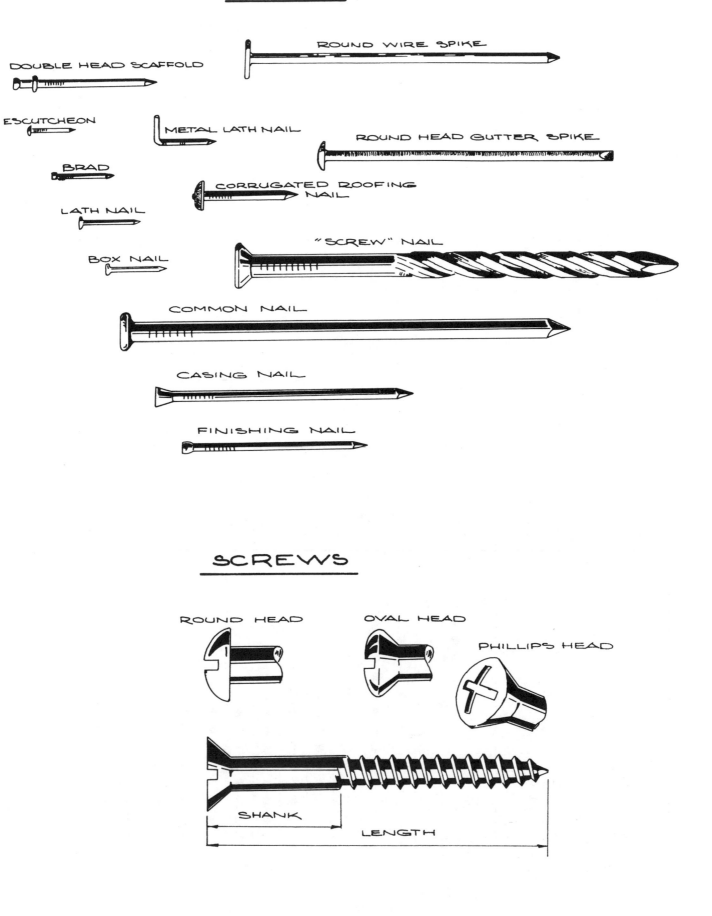

DOUBLE HEAD SCAFFOLD

ROUND WIRE SPIKE

ESCUTCHEON

METAL LATH NAIL

ROUND HEAD GUTTER SPIKE

BRAD

CORRUGATED ROOFING NAIL

LATH NAIL

"SCREW" NAIL

BOX NAIL

COMMON NAIL

CASING NAIL

FINISHING NAIL

SCREWS

ROUND HEAD

OVAL HEAD

PHILLIPS HEAD

SHANK

LENGTH

NAIL SIZE REFERENCE CHART

TYPE		FINISHING			CASING			COMMON			BOX		
SIZE	LGTH.	STD.	GA.	NO/LB.	STD.	GA.	NO/LB.	STD.	GA.	NO/LB.	STD.	GA.	NO/LB.
2d	1"							●	15	800			
3d	1¼"	●	15½	720				●	14	480	●	14½	550
4d	1½"	●	15	525	●	14	400	●	12½	290	●	14	400
5d	1¾"							●	12½	200	●	14	325
6d	2"	●	13	270	●	12½	225	●	11½	170	●	12½	200
7d	2¼"							●	11½	125	●	12½	150
8d	2½"	●	12½	145	●	11½	130	●	10¼	90	●	11½	100
9d	2¾"							●	10¼	70			
10d	3"	●	11½	100	●	10½	90	●	9	60	●	10½	75
12d	3¼"							●	9	45			
16d	3½"				●	10	55	●	8	35	●	10	45
20d	4"							●	6	25	●	9	30
30d	4½"							●	5	20			
40d	5"							●	4	15			
50d	5½"							●	3	10			
60d	6"							●	2	8			

SCREW SIZE REFERENCE CHART

SCREW SIZE	BODY DIA.	1/4	3/8	1/2	5/8	3/4	7/8	1	1¼	1½	1¾	2	2¼	2½	2¾	3	3½	4
0	.060	●																
1	.073	●																
2	.086	●	●	●														
3	.099	●	●	●	●													
4	.112		●	●	●	●												
5	.125		●	●	●	●												
6	.138		●	●	●	●	●	●		●								
7	.151		●	●	●	●	●	●	●	●								
8	.164			●	●	●	●	●	●	●	●	●						
9	.177				●	●	●	●	●	●	●	●	●					
10	.190					●	●	●	●	●	●	●	●	●				
11	.203						●	●	●	●	●	●	●					
12	.216							●	●	●	●	●	●	●				
14	.242							●	●	●	●	●	●	●	●			
16	.268								●	●	●	●	●	●	●	●		
18	.294									●	●	●	●	●	●	●	●	●
20	.320									●	●	●	●	●	●	●	●	●
24	.372																●	●

As soon as the framing of load-bearing walls is completed, the roof may be built. Don't install the finished surface components on your interior walls until after the roof has been placed, as there is neither need nor sense to expose interior finishes to the hazards of the elements. The variety of available paneling, wallboards or other wall surfacings is now so great as to bemuse the perplexed householder with their wide diversity. Therefore, as these items should not be installed at this point, we will not even discuss them until we arrive at the section on interiors.

Now, your walls are up and ready for the construction of the roof, which you can now build to get yourself covered up, and in out of the weather.

CHAPTER VIII

The Roof Of Your Adobe Home

As you may have guessed, you are about to embark upon yet another element of your adobe home, wherein you must choose between several alternate methods of attaining the same ends, namely, putting a roof on your adobe home.

The first roofing decision will be whether to stick to the traditional flat roof, or to change to a pitched roof. We'll tell you right now, that if you want a pitched roof, you can dig up the answers to all your questions by your ownself, as this is another point where we stick with tradition. In fact, we are so in accord with the traditional flat roof on adobe homes, that we won't even discuss the pitched roof. Therefore, those of you who insist upon the use of a pitched roof may as well skip the rest of this section, as there won't be a thing in it for you.

Unless a pitched roof is utilized to provide room for dead air space insulation, or to include an attic, it is darn well expensively built wasted space. Flat roofs can be built with dead air space insulation, and you don't need an attic if your planning has given adequate storage space, so who needs to go to all the trouble of pitching rafters and fancy roofing when it doesn't produce benefits equal to the cost. Some of the detractors of flat roofs insist that they cannot be drained, well, our answer to those folk is quite simply that perhaps they just don't know how to drain anything.

Perhaps we had better define the terminology that we will use in this section, as some may not agree with our usages, and become even more confused. "Roof," as used herein, will refer to the entire complex of components at the top of the home, including structural, decorative, insulative and waterproofing elements. "Ceiling" shall refer to that lower portion of the roof, either above or below the beams or vigas, that is the only portion exposed to view from within the home, and thus has a decorative aspect. The structural elements of the roof are the vigas, beams, rafters or joists that carry the load of the rest of the roof, transferring that load to the load-bearing walls of the home. "Roofing" shall refer to a layer of material, which may or may not be the top element of the roof. Other terms should be self-evident when examined in the context of their usage.

There are several variations in basic construction utilized for the roofs of adobe homes, which may be called the adobe roof, the dead air space roof, and the conventional roof, all of which may be further complicated by using either vigas or conventional joists as the load-carrying structural components. Each of these variations has its own appeal to someone, so we will discuss them all, then as usual, abandon you to make your own decision.

The most traditional roof for adobe homes is, of course, the adobe roof. With a very few changes for the sake of the times, this method can still produce an inexpensive, durable, waterproof roof. In common with all flat roofs on adobe homes, it is not visible from the same level as the home, due to the parapet surrounding the roof, whether the home's style is Pueblo or Territorial. This parapet performs several functions, as it affords roof tiedown, controls drainage points, provides some structural benefits, and is also quite decorative. The parapet may extend from one to two, or even three feet above the ceiling of the house, depending upon the roof type employed, the structural elements used, and the architectural criteria.

Whatever the roof type, the structural members will rest upon the roof lintel, perimeter beam or top plate which has already been installed on top of all the load-bearing walls. Of course, at the time of that installation, you took great care to assure that the tops of these beams were dead level with each other throughout. These structural members may be vigas, beams, or conventional wood joists. The traditional viga is a six or eight inch diameter tree-trunk, which has been trimmed, debarked and seasoned. It is most often left its natural color, then varnished. The viga is raised, positioned, and laid in place across the two load-bearing walls at the measured distance from the next viga. This distance will vary, from about sixteen inches to perhaps thirty inches, depending upon the actual diameter of the viga, the clear span required, and the weight of the rest of the roof. The viga is then secured to the top plate with a throughbolt to hold it in place. The length of the viga depends upon the clear span needed, plus whatever length projects beyond the face of the outside wall. If it is to support a portal roof, then it must project to the lintel atop the portal columns, if not, it may exend from two to three feet beyond the outside face of the wall, for effective decoration.

The viga may be flattened on top along the distance that the rest of the roof, including the ceiling, will bear on it. The bottom of the viga should be flattened only where it bears upon the wall, and the projecting end is left full round. Some of the traditionalists insist that a hole must be bored on top of the viga at the exposed end, so that oil or other preservative may periodically be poured into the top of the viga to protect it from rotting. However, we see little benefit in this if the coat of varnish is maintained, and reapplied to control the development of checking

or cracking. A square or rectangular beam may be used instead of the viga, erected and secured in the same fashion. There are some who also call a squared-off beam a viga, which is a misnomer to the traditionalist, who insists that only the full-round trunk may be termed a viga, and that the squared-off item is a beam. The squared-off beam is only rarely encountered in Pueblo style adobe homes, but is utilized frequently in the Territorial styling.

After the vigas have been positioned and secured, the ceiling is laid atop them and nailed down. The traditional ceiling is made up of thin boards laid in a herringbone pattern; i.e., boards are laid at a diagonal across the space between two or more vigas, and at the opposite diagonal across the next space. The boards are generally only varnished, although some few have been stained to either match or contrast the vigas. This narrow herringbone pattern of boards is a whole lot of hand work, but the results may be worth it to you. If not, plywood is now on the market with so many different face textures that you can surely find one that would be attractive to you for a ceiling over the vigas. Select the facing you like, lay the 4x8 sheets over the vigas and nail them down. On top of the ceiling, a moisture barrier of the same polyethylene plastic film you used under the floor is rolled out and smoothed. Then, over the moisture barrier, we at last get to the meat of this roof type, the adobe soil.

The adobe soil is mixed to the same proportions as were all the other adobe components of the home, then deposited in layers across the roof area and compacted. The final compacted thickness of the roofing adobe should be at least eight inches to offer some mass effect. Over the top of the adobe is then spread a layer of hot roofing asphalt, which is sprinkled with pea gravel. Right after the vigas had been laid, the adobe block parapet wall was to have been completed to its full height, and the canales, or roof drains installed. The canales are located about every 10 to 15 feet on the side of the roof's low point. The top surface of the roof is to be sloped at about one-quarter inch per foot from the high side to the low side, where the canales will drain all water off the roof. Most builders like to place a small concrete pad against the base of the house wall right under each canale, so that the flow of runoff water from the roof will not erode the soil at the base of the wall.

The air space roof is, in effect, a double roof with an enclosed air space between the layers. Up to and including the polyethylene plastic moisture barrier, the air space roof method may be built identically to the adobe roof. Above the moisture barrier is to be installed a layer of insulating material, of the type and thickness of your preference. Then, above the insulation is an air space one to two feet high, which is vented through the parapet wall. The vent is a short section of 4" tile, with a fine-mesh screen over the inside end to prevent the entrance of birds, bats, belfries or other objectionable wildlife. At the top of the air space is a layer of wood sheathing, which is covered by a layer of roofing tar paper, which is also covered with a layer of hot roofing asphalt sprinkled with pea gravel. The parapet wall and canales are the same for all of the roof types, except that the height may vary.

Another roof type may be built, very similar to the preceding method, except that no air space is provided, the layer of sheathing being located right on top of the insulation, but supported over it so that the insulation is not compressed.

One of the major differences between these roof styles and the conventional roof type is that, in the conventional roof, the ceiling is attached below the joists instead of above vigas or beams. The wood joists are laid across the load-bearing walls and nailed to the top plates. The size of the joists and the spacing between them is also dictated by the length of clear span, and the roof type selected. The polyethylene moisture barrier is laid between the joists and the insulation, which may be laid in batts in the space between joists. The rest of the roof may be any type set out herein, or any combination of those types. There are some people who even combine the joist and viga types in their homes, as they like the vigas in the living room, but prefer the suspended ceiling in other rooms.

So now you have it, the walls are up, the roof is on, and windows and doors are set into their openings, and the house is closed up. At least part of the utilities are already installed, as they had to be located either in walls, in or under the floor, and through the foundation. It sounds so very simple to say that all you have to do now, is finish the utilities, complete the interior, install your heating plant, move in your appliances and furniture, and start living.

As you well know by now, it will not be nearly that simple, as the fact that there are a few more sections left to this book betrays.

CHAPTER IX

Heating Your Adobe Home

The heating plant may be the largest single-unit cash outlay for your adobe home. It is no place to skimp on size or price, although some economies can be realized through doing part or all of the installation yourself. The proper sizing of a heating plant is a quite technical affair, and should be done with extreme accuracy for optimum results. An under-sized plant will never be able to adequately heat your home, and will be uncomfortable and unhealthy. An over-sized plant is one of the few aspects of your home where "bigger is better" is not true. The fuel bills resulting from a too-large heating plant will make you wince every time one arrives.

Since you must either purchase or contract your heating plant in any case, do it through a professional heating contractor or supplier who will perform the detailed heat-loss calculations for you. Almost every aspect of your home enters into these calculations, and varies considerably for each individual home. Thus, we see no point in setting forth two tons of data to permit everyone reading this book to determine these needs, when you have to go to the professional to purchase the unit anyhow. You may even decide to contract the complete installation, which lays the onus of adequacy completely upon the contractor. If you do this, get the contract written in terms of guaranteed results, not an agreement to supply "x" equipment. If you happen to run onto one of those fringe-area types who does his calculations by the "shotgun" method just walk away from him, fast. Here, as with any other purchased or contracted item, check out the en-

tire local market, especially as regards reliability or reputation. A competent firm will not object to answering questions or being checked out, and it's much better to be safe than sorry, even if that is a cliché. You can specify that the end results of the heating plant installation must meet the comfort conditions of the National Warm Air Heating and Air Conditioning Association, and if the contractor won't guarantee this in writing, walk away. These comfort conditions demand a system that provides:

An inside temperature of 70 degress when the outside temperature is 0 degrees or below.

Floor temperatures of 68-70 degrees, even at outside corners.

Temperatures should not vary more than 1½ degrees between firing cycles or on-off periods of burners.

Temperature variation from floor level to the sitting zone at 30 inches above the floor should not be more than 2½ degrees when outside temperature is 30, and not more than 4 degrees when outside temperatures is 0.

The temperature of a slab floor should not exceed 85.

You must decide on the basic system to be used in the heating plant, and again, there is considerable variety. The systems available include warm air, hot water, steam, or heat pumps. Most of these types can be obtained with different fuel sources, as gas, oil, or electricity. The fuel source may also influence your choice of heating system, as you can obviously use only

FORCED WARM-AIR HEATING PLANTS

TYPICAL FURNACE LAYOUT

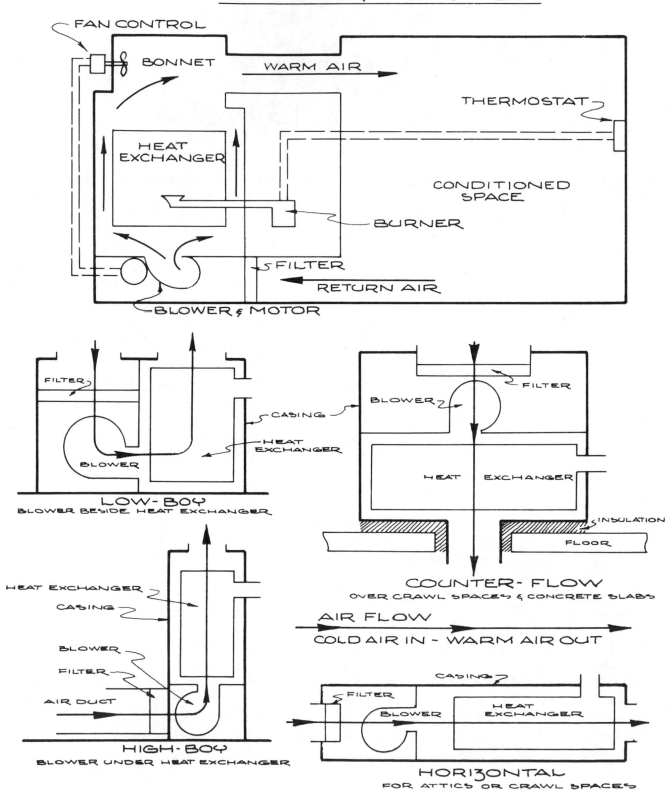

FAN CONTROL

BONNET

WARM AIR

THERMOSTAT

HEAT EXCHANGER

CONDITIONED SPACE

BURNER

FILTER

RETURN AIR

BLOWER & MOTOR

FILTER

CASING

HEAT EXCHANGER

BLOWER

LOW-BOY
BLOWER BESIDE HEAT EXCHANGER

BLOWER

FILTER

HEAT EXCHANGER

INSULATION

FLOOR

COUNTER-FLOW
OVER CRAWL SPACES & CONCRETE SLABS

AIR FLOW

COLD AIR IN — WARM AIR OUT

HEAT EXCHANGER

CASING

BLOWER

FILTER

AIR DUCT

HIGH-BOY
BLOWER UNDER HEAT EXCHANGER

CASING

FILTER

BLOWER

HEAT EXCHANGER

HORIZONTAL
FOR ATTICS OR CRAWL SPACES

FORCED WARM-AIR HEATING PLANTS

DISTRIBUTION SYSTEMS

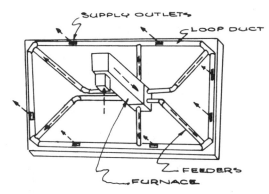

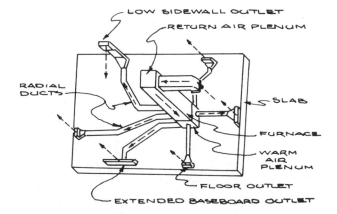

PERIMETER-LOOP TYPE

Supply Outlets
Loop Duct
Feeders
Furnace

PERIMETER-RADIAL TYPE

Low Sidewall Outlet
Return Air Plenum
Radial Ducts
Slab
Furnace
Warm Air Plenum
Floor Outlet
Extended Baseboard Outlet

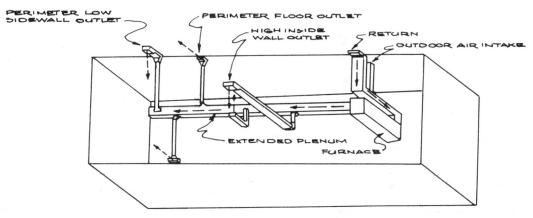

Perimeter Low Sidewall Outlet
Perimeter Floor Outlet
High Inside Wall Outlet
Return
Outdoor Air Intake
Extended Plenum
Furnace

EXTENDED PLENUM TYPE

FEEDER DUCT DIAMETERS

BTUH/FEEDER	DUCT LENGTH	
	0'-15'	16'-30'
1,000 - 8,000	6"	6"
8,000 - 9,000	6"	7"
9,000 - 11,000	7"	7"
11,000 - 12,000	7"	8"
12,000 - 13,000	7"	8"
13,000 - 17,000	8"	8"

DUCTS IN SLABS

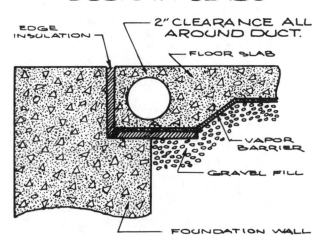

Edge Insulation
2" Clearance All Around Duct.
Floor Slab
Vapor Barrier
Gravel Fill
Foundation Wall

FORCED WARM-AIR HEATING SYSTEMS

ROOM DIFFUSER AREAS

HEAT LOSS OF ROOM, BTUH	LENGTH OF FEEDER	SQUARE INCHES - ROOM DIFFUSER FREE AREA FEEDER DUCT OF ROOM + ½ PERIMETER DUCT, FT.						
		0'-9'	10'-19'	20'-29'	30'-39'	40'-49'	50'-59'	60'-69'
0 - 4,000	2'-10'	20						
	10'-20'	23	18	18				
	20'-30'	27	21	21				
4,000 - 6,000	2'-10'	32	27	23	18			
	10'-20'	36	31	26	21	16	16	
	20'-30'	42	36	30	24	18		
6,000 - 8,000	2'-10'	43	39	34	29	25	20	
	10'-20'	49	44	39	34	29	24	19
	20'-30'	57	51	45	39	33	27	21
8,000 - 10,000	2'-10'	55	50	45	41	36	32	27
	10'-20'	61	56	51	46	41	36	31
	20'-30'	72	66	60	54	48	42	36
10,000 - 12,000	2'-10'	66	61	57	52	48	43	38
	10'-20'	73	68	63	58	53	48	43
	20'-30'	86	80	74	68	62	56	50
12,000 - 14,000	2'-10'	77	72	68	63	59	54	50
	10'-20'	86	81	76	71	66	61	56
	20'-30'	101	95	89	83	77	71	65
14,000 - 16,000	2'-10'	88	84	79	75	70	66	61
	10'-20'	99	94	89	84	79	74	69
	20'-30'	116	110	104	98	92	86	80
16,000 - 18,000	2'-10'	100	95	91	86	82	77	72
	10'-20'	111	106	101	96	91	86	81
	20'-30'	131	125	119	113	107	101	95
18,000 - 20,000	2'-10'	111	106	102	97	93	88	84
	10'-20'	123	118	113	108	103	98	93
	20'-30'	145	139	133	127	121	115	109
20,000 - 22,000	2'-10'	122	118	113	109	104	100	95
	10'-20'	135	130	125	120	116	110	105
	20'-30'	160	154	148	142	136	130	124
22,000 - 24,000	2'-10'	134	129	125	120	116	111	106
	10'-20'	148	143	138	133	128	123	118
	20'-30'	175	169	163	157	151	145	139
24,000 - 26,000	2'-10'	145	140	136	131	127	122	118
	10'-20'	161	156	151	146	141	136	131
	20'-30'	190	184	178	172	166	160	154
26,000 - 28,000	2'-10'	156	151	147	142	138	133	129
	10'-20'	174	168	164	158	154	148	144
	20'-30'	205	199	193	187	181	175	169
28,000 - 30,000	2'-10'	168	163	159	154	150	145	141
	10'-20'	186	181	176	171	166	161	156
	20'-30'	220	214	208	202	196	190	184
30,000 - 32,000	2'-10'	179	174	170	165	161	156	152
	10'-20'	198	194	188	184	178	174	168
	20'-30'	234	228	222	216	210	204	198
32,000 - 34,000	2'-10'	190	185	182	176	173	167	164
	10'-20'	211	206	201	196	191	186	181
	20'-30'	249	243	237	231	225	219	213

6 IN. DIA. DUCTS - HEAT DELIVERY

NO. OF ELBOWS	CAP.	PIPE LENGTH FROM BONNET TO DIFFUSER, FT.									
		35	40	45	50	55	60	65	70	75	80
0	BTUH				8700	8060	7460	6920	6430	5960	5550
	CFM				127.7	124.8	122.3	119.7	117.4	115.0	113.0
1	BTUH			8620	8000	7430	6900	6400	5930	5500	5100
	CFM			122.8	120.0	117.6	115.3	113.0	111.0	109.0	107.3
2	BTUH		8600	7960	7390	6860	6380	5940	5530	5150	4800
	CFM		118.5	116.2	114.0	112.0	110.0	107.8	106.0	104.5	103.0
3	BTUH	8640	8020	7450	6950	6460	6020	5600	5200	4850	4500
	CFM	114.0	112.0	110.0	108.2	106.5	104.7	103.0	101.4	99.6	98.0

a fuel that is available at reasonable cost in your vicinity. Steam systems, heat pumps and hot water systems are all excellent modern types, but all share the same disadvantage, in that they are considerably more expensive than the warm air systems. As evidence of this, over 75% of current housing construction in this country uses warm air heating, so we will bow to the majority and discuss this system.

Among the benefits of warm air heating cited by its advocates, perhaps the prime consideration is that the cost may be 20% less than that of an equal quality hot water system. Other benefits ascribed to warm air systems include rapid heat delivery or cut-off, good air filtration, controlled humidity, continual air circulation, and adaptability to the later addition of air conditioning. The warm air system of today has been greatly improved from the obsolete units of yesteryear. The entire system is smaller and more efficient, affording adequate heating at lower cost, especially when fueled with natural gas.

The selection of fuel source for your heating system depends upon the local availability and cost of the alternatives. Natural gas is the most convenient and sometimes the most economic heating fuel, but it is not always available at all home-sites. To demonstrate comparative fuel cost, we have to dissertate a bit upon standards. A standard unit of measurement in the heating industry is the BTU, or British Thermal Unit, which is that quantity of heat required to raise the temperature of one pound of pure water by one degree Fahrenheit at mean sea level. The average home may require from 6 to 12 BTUs per hour to heat each cubic foot of space inside the home. This can lead to some very large figures in BTUs, so the Therm has been adopted to indicate 100,000 BTUs.

The cost of each fuel varies with locality and demand, but the following data is an average, considering the relative efficiencies of these fuels.

Fuel	Cost per Therm
No. 2 Fuel Oil	13½¢
Electricity	44¢ to 73¢
Natural Gas	8¢ to 16¢

We have ignored such fuels as coal, propane or butane gas, kerosene, coke, and others because of various drawbacks; i.e., coal is dirty, the liquefied petroleum gases, propane or butane, can be very hazardous, and kerosene is inefficient. Therefore, the availability of various fuels to the site becomes yet another point to be considered when you start looking around for a place to build your adobe home.

The forced warm air heating system has become so adaptable that the furnace unit may now be located anywhere in the home, from a closet to a utility room or attic, rather than lurking in the center of a basement, as the old, obsolete systems required. The new furnaces are small, compact, complete units which may be placed quite close to combustible walls with safety. The major types of forced warm air furnaces are the standard type for basement installation, the counterflow type for use in a main floor closet or utility room, and the horizontal type for installation in a crawl space or attic. The reduced furnace sizes and the miniaturization of ductwork now offer the full use of any area of the home without interference from the components of the heating system.

A fairly recent development in forced warm air heating is the perimeter system. Older heat systems utilized warm air registers on inside walls and cold air returns on outside walls. The perimeter system eliminates cold air return ductwork and releases warm air at the place where the heat is lost. As from 65% to 80% of a home's heat loss is at outside walls near windows, placing diffusers at the base of these areas warms the outside walls, diminishing the entrance of cold air and thus reducing drafts. With this system, the diffusers, which are registers that discharge warm air in a fan effect, must be placed in the floor, rather than in baseboards or walls. The cold air return ductwork is no longer needed, as air supply for the blower may come from small entry grilles, which can be located at almost any convenient point.

One of the best floor diffusers for a perimeter system is a 2″ x 14″ type, which can deliver as much as 10,000 BTU. For rooms with greater heat losses, use two or more of the same diffusers, rather than one larger one, for better heat distribution and circulation.

There are three basic types of forced warm air perimeter heating systems, which differ almost entirely in variations of the ductwork. The radial perimeter system has small, round ducts leading from the furnace directly to each diffuser. The extended plenum perimeter system has one or more large rectangular ducts from which individual ducts run to the diffusers. The radial loop perimeter system has the same direct ducts as the radial system, with the addition of a separate duct running completely around the perimeter. The radial system is best utilized in small, compact homes, where the individual ducts will be comparatively short. The extended plenum system is most efficient for larger homes, where some of the diffusers may be more than 25 feet from the furnace. The radial loop system is intended for use in slab-on-grade homes, where the radial ducts are embedded in the slab, and the perimeter loop gives off extra heat at the slab edge.

We have not discussed gravity warm air systems, floor furnaces or resistance heaters, as these are simply not adequate for average home heating, when considering the better products that are now available at comparable costs. You may consider these items, if your area has extremely mild winters, but consider that even southern Florida has had some bad winters, and that it's too late to install heating plants when the thermometer's mercury has dropped down into the bulb to hide.

CHAPTER X

Electric Power In Your Adobe Home

The general public is probably more ignorant about the vagaries and characteristics of electric power than any other aspect of their daily lives. This is rather perplexing, when it is considered how intimately our lives are intertwined with that hot juice, and the vast quantities of the stuff that are consumed daily by each one of us. Take Mr. Non-Existant Average Man, who may know the batting average of every player since Ty Cobb, the yards gained or won-lost record of all coaches since Knute Rockne, the horsepower of every V8 that ever came out of Detroit, or even all about the care and feeding of roses, and ask this man, or woman, some simple questions about electricity. His response to a query on ergs, ohms, watts, volts, AC, DC, cycles, amps and suchlike may be to announce to all and sundry that you are some kind of a nut.

All that most of us know about electricity is that it comes out of that little outlet on the wall, and that if you plug a light or appliance into that outlet, well, most of the time it works. We will always remember the day we were in the home of a little old lady who had stuffed bits of cotton into the prong-holes of all of her unused electric outlets, as she was convinced that the stuff would otherwise leak out all over her immaculate floors. There are some quite thorny problems in electrical research and theory, but we will not become involved in any of that, and shall just briefly discuss the practical aspects of electric power for your adobe home.

The two basic flows of electricity are alternating current, or AC, and direct current, or DC.

Direct current is a smooth, even flow of electric current produced by batteries or generators, but is not well adaptable to transmission at low voltages. AC is produced, either by conversion from DC or directly, from an alternator, and is readily transmitted and may be raised or lowered in voltage through transformers. Almost all of the domestic electric distribution in this country is AC, so we will now ignore DC, and continue.

Alternating current flows through a circuit in a wave form, from zero to peak voltage in one direction, then from zero to peak in the opposite direction. Thus, the current alternates its flow in cycles, which in this country are set at 60 cycles per second for domestic distribution. For illustration, let's trace the path of an electric current from the generating station to your light bulb. Some of the modern generating stations produce power in a range from 11,000 to 14,000 volts. Put through a transformer, this current is boosted to from 23,000 to 275,000 or more volts for long-distance transmission. This voltage boost is done as, the higher the voltage, the lower is the current in amperes for a given load, and thus lessening the conductor size required. As the transmission line reaches its destination, it is stepped down in a substation, or primary distribution point, to voltages ranging between 2,500 and 15,000. It then flows to a secondary distribution point, or transformer, where it is dropped to 115 to 230 volts, and sent down the line to your home, where it flows through your meter, then a fuse or circuit box, emerges from an outlet into your lamp cord, heats the element in the bulb, and produces the light by which you may be reading this book.

The various transmission and distribution methods and voltages may have no interest for you, but they affect the type of residential electric service which may be available at your home-site, and your home's wiring will have to conform to whichever systems and voltages the local electric utility may have for domestic service at your site. The four basic residential electric power systems are: the two-wire, 115 volt system; the three-wire single-phase, 115-230 volt system; the four-wire, three-phase, 120-208 volts, and the three-wire single-phase, 120-208 volt systems. Therefore, another consideration when selecting your home-site is to determine what power system is available at the site, as you are a prisoner of the public utility in that respect.

The two-wire, 115 volt system is the oldest of this group, and at one time, was the only power system given for domestic use. It is now generally considered to be obsolete, although it may still be the only system available in some remote areas. It is not considered adequate for modern residential service demands, but will be sufficient for a mountain cabin or the like. This system has two wires which come from the nearest transformer, pass through the watt-hour meter, the circuit or fuse box, and lead into individual circuits serving the home. One of these wires, called the ground wire, has white or gray colored insulation, and may be connected to a nearby water pipe. The other wire, called the hot wire, has black insulation. The ground wire is not dead, but both wires are needed to complete the circuit, so the hot wire has all the switches and fuses on it for control purposes. The main switch and fuse are placed in the same steel box, so that opening the switch or blowing the fuse cuts off all power into the home. Near this, or even in the same box, are the fuses of all of the individual circuits serving the home. Thus, an overload on one circuit blows its own fuse, and yet permits power to continue into all of the other circuits.

Balance the loads on your circuits, and pro-

vide enough circuits to serve all of the anticipated power demands in your home. There are three pages of tables on circuitry and wiring needs inserted in this section, so you should be able to lay out your circuitry by studying them, and resolving the data to fit your own needs. Don't try to save money by cutting down on circuits, try to balance each circuit load at around 1,200 watts total demand, as overloading a circuit is not only dangerous, but requires more amperage to fill the demand, and that bounces your power bill up considerably. Another point to be kept in mind is that most utility firms are somewhat reluctant to hook their power up to non-professionally wired homes, so you may get some static from them unless you contact them beforehand, perhaps at the time you first inquire as to the power system availability. They may even demand to inspect your wiring, and although you may think this is officious, it is done to protect you and yours, so play it cool and don't blow your own fuses.

The three-wire, single-phase, 115-230 volt system is much more adaptable to the needs of the modern home, in that it provides 115 volt service for all usual electric service, and also 230 volts for heavy appliances such as stoves or air conditioners, etc. The center of the three wires is the neutral, with white or gray insulation, and must be grounded. Between this neutral and either black wire is 115 volts. The needed 115 volt branch circuits are balanced so that each half of the system carries the same approximate total load. A circuit across both black wires produces 230 volts for heavy current-demand appliances. The virtue of the higher voltage is that it reduces the current in amperes, and heat losses and overload hazard are therefore also reduced. This benefit is further illustrated when it is understood that electric service bills are all based upon consumption of kilowatt-hours of electric service. A kilowatt is 1,000 watts, and the watt is the measure of the rate of doing work, being equal to volts times amperes. Therefore, in any practical combination of voltage times amperes that equal the same watts, the formula of the higher voltage necessarily gives lower amperes, with the resultant lower heat losses, line current and voltage drops.

The four-wire, three-phase, 120-208 volt system has long been in use in industry, but only recently has come into demand in domestic service with the advent of central air conditioning units, and their large horsepower requirements. Three-phase power indicates that, rather than one cycle of voltage pulsing in the line every 1/60th of a second, there are three such pulses, as three phases, or cycles, of voltage flow from the generator. Thus, three-phase power provides a smoother flow of energy for greater efficiency in electric motors.

In this system, a four-wire cable leads into the house from the street line. One of these wires, again the grounded neutral, has white insulation, and the other three hot lines have red insulation. The normal circuits for lighting and minor appliances are single-phase 120 volts, and are picked off between the neutral and any of the red wires. For slightly heavier loads, such as freezers, stoves or small unit air conditioners, separate circuits of single-phase 208 volts may be taken off from any two red wires. Then, for the heavy loads of larger electric motors, such as central unit air conditioners, a circuit of all three of the red wires gives three-phase 208 volt service. A separate return or neutral wire is not needed with three-phase circuits on a motor load.

The three-wire, single-phase, 120-208 volt service is an adaptation of the four-wire three-phase system, as there are some heavy load areas where only the three-phase system is available from the company's service lines. If there is no need in the home for three-phase power, rather than running the entire four-wire service, only a neutral and two red wires are led into the home's system. From this service, either single-phase 120 or 208 volts are obtained from the neutral and one red wire, or both red wires, respectively.

When laying out your circuit needs during the planning period, balance the total loads on each circuit insofar as possible. Don't wind up with one circuit loaded with only 200 watts and another with a total load of several thousand watts. The only area where theoretical circuit overload is permissible is with incompatible use items. That is, a room air conditioner and a space heater in the same room could be wired into the same circuit, as it is a bit unlikely that both items would be in use at the same time.

The actual wiring of your adobe home should be done to conform to the National Electrical Code for your own safety. Also, almost all of the local building codes are based upon that Code, but check on the local code, as it may contain some variations. In fact, check all of the local codes while you are still in the planning stage, as it is a bit easier to conform at that time rather than after you have already completed an illegal, and possibly hazardous, installation. The local electric utility company can be the source of some excellent advice on your internal wiring, but they will take no responsibility for anything past the meter. Up to and including the meter, it's their baby, but from that point on, it's strictly up to you. The tables in this section show some recommended wire sizes, but may not be true in unusual circumstances. Plan enough circuits so that the home will have extra load capability available for some unanticipated future usage, as you can't really be sure what appliances, tools or motors you may purchase in the future. Also check on the manufacturer's recommendations regarding voltage, wiring or circuitry for any and all large appliances, heaters, tools, etc. Remember that there is a great deal of truth in that sage old rule, "When in doubt, read the instructions."

All of your wiring runs will be either cable or conduit, depending on the location of the wiring and the conditions of the local code. The types most used for residential construction include nonmetallic sheathed cable, BX steel-armored cable, and thin-wall steel conduit.

Nonmetallic sheathed cable, also known as loom cable from the woven appearance of the outer sheath, may have two or three insulated wires, with or without a bare ground wire, laid together in a common sheath. It is available in a variety of wire sizes and sheath materials, and

TYPICAL WIRING SYSTEMS
RESIDENTIAL USE

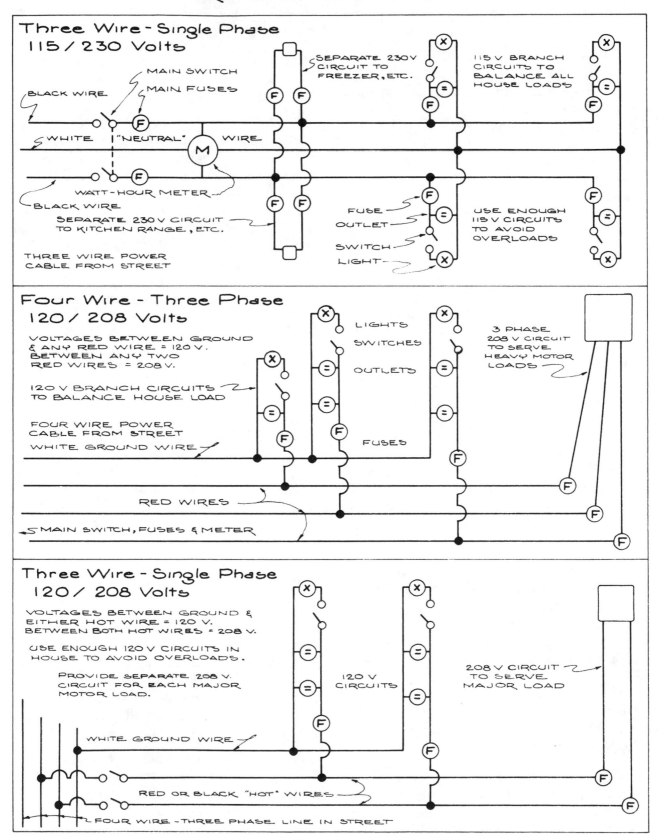

Three Wire - Single Phase 115/230 Volts

BLACK WIRE

MAIN SWITCH
MAIN FUSES

WHITE "NEUTRAL" WIRE

WATT-HOUR METER

BLACK WIRE

Separate 230 V CIRCUIT TO FREEZER, ETC.

115 V BRANCH CIRCUITS TO BALANCE ALL HOUSE LOADS

FUSE
OUTLET
SWITCH
LIGHT

USE ENOUGH 115 V CIRCUITS TO AVOID OVERLOADS

SEPARATE 230 V CIRCUIT TO KITCHEN RANGE, ETC.

THREE WIRE POWER CABLE FROM STREET

Four Wire - Three Phase 120/208 Volts

VOLTAGES BETWEEN GROUND & ANY RED WIRE = 120 V. BETWEEN ANY TWO RED WIRES = 208 V.

120 V BRANCH CIRCUITS TO BALANCE HOUSE LOAD

FOUR WIRE POWER CABLE FROM STREET

WHITE GROUND WIRE

RED WIRES

MAIN SWITCH, FUSES & METER

LIGHTS
SWITCHES
OUTLETS
FUSES

3 PHASE 208 V CIRCUIT TO SERVE HEAVY MOTOR LOADS

Three Wire - Single Phase 120/208 Volts

VOLTAGES BETWEEN GROUND & EITHER HOT WIRE = 120 V. BETWEEN BOTH HOT WIRES = 208 V.

USE ENOUGH 120 V CIRCUITS IN HOUSE TO AVOID OVERLOADS.

PROVIDE SEPARATE 208 V. CIRCUIT FOR EACH MAJOR MOTOR LOAD.

WHITE GROUND WIRE

RED OR BLACK "HOT" WIRES

FOUR WIRE - THREE PHASE LINE IN STREET

120 V CIRCUITS

208 V CIRCUIT TO SERVE MAJOR LOAD

RESIDENTIAL WIRING NEEDS

UNIT	WATTS	CIRC.	VOLTS	WIRE	FUSE	TYPE	REMARKS
KITCHEN :							
RANGE	12,000	10 kw	120/240	3 #6	50A	A	SINGLE CIRCUIT
OVEN	4,500	6 kw	120/240	3 #10	30A	A	} MAY BE DIRECT-CONNECTED
RANGE TOP	6,000	6 kw	120/240	3 #10	30A	A	
RANGE TOP	3,300	4 kw	120/240	3 #12	20A	A	
DISHWASHER	1,200	2 kw	120	2 #12	20A	B	} MAY BE DIRECT-CONNECTED ON SAME CIRCUIT
DISPOSAL U.	300	2 kw	120	2 #12	20A	B	
BROILER	1500	2 kw	120	2 #12	20A	B,C	} USE ONLY ONE SUCH UNIT ON SAME CIRCUIT AT ONE TIME
FRYER	1300	2 kw	120	2 #12	20A	B,C	
COFFEEPOT	1000	2 kw	120	2 #12	20A	B,C	
REFRIGERATOR	300	2 kw	120	2 #12	20A	B,C	} SEPARATE CIRCUIT TO SERVE ONLY THESE TWO UNITS.
FREEZER	350	2 kw	120	2 #12	20A	B,C	
LAUNDRY :							
WASHER	1200	2 kw	120	2 #12	20A	B	SEPARATE CIRCUIT
DRYER	5000	6 kw	120/240	3 #10	30A	A	GROUND
IRONER	1650	2 kw	120	2 #12	20A	B	GROUND
HAND IRON	1000	2 kw	120	2 #12	20A	C	
WATER HEATER	3000					A	CONSULT UTILITY CO.
GENERAL :							
WORKSHOP	1500	2 kw	120	2 #12	20A	A,B,C	SEPARATE CIRCUITS
PORT. HEATER	1300	2 kw	120	2 #12	20A	C	NOT WITH OTHER HEAVY USE
TELEVISION	300	2 kw	120	2 #12	20A	C	NOT WITH APPLIANCES
PORT. LIGHTING	1200	2 kw	120	2 #12	20A	C	ONE CIRCUIT PER 500 SQ. FT.
MISC. :							
FIXED LIGHTING	1200	2 kw	120	2 #12	20A	–	ONE CIRCUIT PER 1200 WATTS
AIR COND. (3/4 hp)	1200	2 kw	120	2 #12	20A	B	
AIR COND. (1½ hp)	2400	4 kw	120/240	3 #12	20A	A	
CENT. AIR COND.	5000	6 kw	120/240			A	CONSULT MFGR.
SUMP PUMP	300	2 kw	120	2 #12	20A	C	
HEATING PLANT	600	2 kw	120	2 #12	20A	–	SINGLE CIRCUIT-DIRECT
BATH HEATER	1500	2 kw	120	2 #12	20A		DIRECT-CONNECTED
VENT. FANS	300	2 kw	120	2 #12	20A	B	

TYPE OF OUTLET

A - SPECIAL PURPOSE

B - PARALLEL GROUNDING

C - PARALLEL

TYPICAL RESIDENTIAL ELECTRICAL CIRCUITS

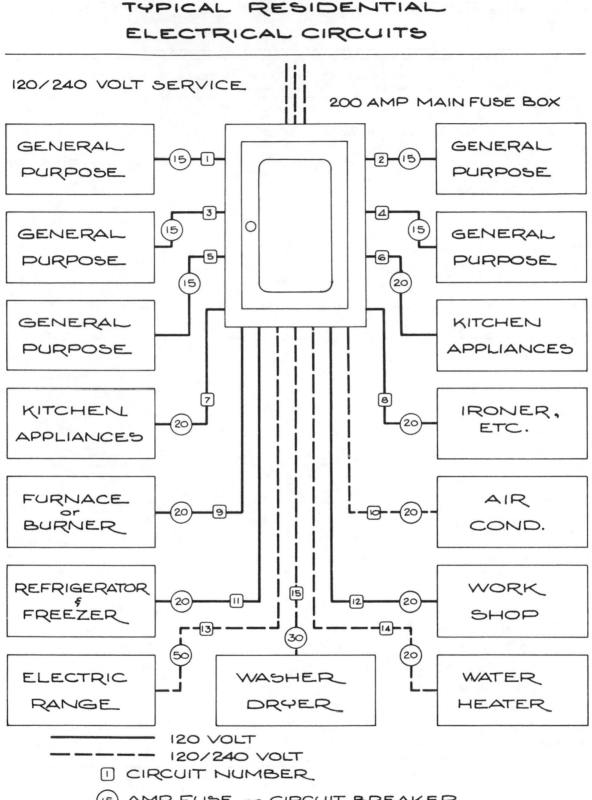

120/240 VOLT SERVICE

200 AMP MAIN FUSE BOX

GENERAL PURPOSE — ⑮ ① · ② ⑮ — GENERAL PURPOSE

GENERAL PURPOSE — ⑮ ③ · ④ ⑮ — GENERAL PURPOSE

GENERAL PURPOSE — ⑮ ⑤ · ⑥ ⑳ — KITCHEN APPLIANCES

KITCHEN APPLIANCES — ⑳ ⑦ · ⑧ ⑳ — IRONER, ETC.

FURNACE or BURNER — ⑳ ⑨ · ⑩ ⑳ — AIR COND.

REFRIGERATOR & FREEZER — ⑳ ⑪ · ⑮ · ⑫ ⑳ — WORK SHOP

ELECTRIC RANGE — ㊿ ⑬ · ㉚ · ⑭ ⑳ — WATER HEATER

WASHER DRYER

———————— 120 VOLT

- - - - - - - - 120/240 VOLT

① CIRCUIT NUMBER

⑮ AMP FUSE or CIRCUIT BREAKER

TYPICAL LAYOUT ABOVE FOR COMPARISON ONLY.
CIRCUITRY NEEDS MUST BE BASED ON ACTUAL
INDIVIDUAL SERVICE REQUIREMENTS.

in rolls from 25 to 250 feet of cable. This cable is inexpensive, flexible, easily cut and handled, and may be secured with U-nails to any wood surface. However, it is prohibited in some uses by various building codes.

BX steel-armored cable may contain two or three insulated wires, perhaps also a bare ground wire, which are encased in a cable of spiral-wound thin steel. It is available in a variety of wire sizes in rolls of from 25 to 250 feet. It is flexible and very tough, and we are not aware of any building codes that prohibit its use. It is more expensive and harder to cut than loom cable, but offers greater protection to the wiring, so we recommend that it be used for all easily accessible wiring.

Thin-wall conduit is galvanized steel pipe, available in standard ten foot lengths in various diameters. It is a bit harder to work than cables, but provides neat and fireproof runs, and in fact is required throughout by some building codes. The wiring is not included with the conduit, but must be pulled through it during or after conduit installation with the aid of a snake, or steel tape. Conduit should be used wherever the run is through adobe walls, under or in floor slabs, or any other inaccessible or hazardous area. Its particular virtues to the do-it-yourselfer are its greater safety and the ability to remove, repair or replace the wiring without disturbing the run of the conduit, which could save you the labor of tearing out a floor or wall to get at it.

While you are planning your wiring, don't forget "Old Ma Bell," as you will most probably want one or more telephones in your adobe home. Decide where you will want these telephones located for optimum use, then go see the local phone company's service representative, who will assist you in determining how, where, what, or if for locating the telephone wiring. A great many of the telephone companies will insist on doing all of this wiring themselves, so contact them early to avoid conflicts.

Of course, at the end of a great many of your electric power circuits, you will install light fixtures. The two most commonly used electric light sources are incandescent bulbs or fluorescent tubes. The variety of sizes and types of light fixtures is awesome, so we will offer just a brief discussion of the basics of the two sources.

Incandescent bulbs are available in an extreme variety of sizes, shapes, and colors, and from 10 to 1,500 watts. The standard base is used up to 300 watts, and the large, or mogul, base is used for 300 watts or larger bulbs. Most incandescent bulbs are now inside-frosted, so that the surface of the bulb is the light source, rather than the hot filament within. The advantages of incandescent bulbs include the ability to focus or point the light over a selected area, the interchangeability of the same base-size bulbs to different wattages to either increase or decrease the concentration of light, and the comparatively lower cost of the bulbs and fixtures.

Fluorescent lamps are tubular light sources which provide higher efficiency, cooler temperatures and longer service life than do incandescent lamps with the same quantity of illumination. The fluorescents range from 4 to 100 watts, and from 6″ to 96″ long. They all require a control device called a ballast and perhaps a starter, and the special fixtures into which they are inserted. The benefits of these tubes are that they provide a line of light, which can be utilized with multiple fixtures to eliminate shadows, they give off three to four times as much light per watt of electricity as do incandescents, with less heat, and usually last from seven to ten times longer before burning out.

The available sizes, types and colors in both types offer the opportunity to mix or blend lighting to solve any need, and fixtures will be chosen for both functional and decorative use, so we leave that all up to you.

CHAPTER XI

Plumbing In Your Adobe Home

There will be three separate piping systems in your home, being one each for cold water, hot water, and wastewater. There should be no cross-connections between these systems, most particularly from the wastewater to either of the other systems. It is quite obvious that raw sewage is dangerous to your health, and must not be allowed to contact any potable water.

Water is piped into your home, is consumed or used in a variety of ways, and is then piped out of the home for disposal. This water has to come from somewhere, and also is sent to some destination. These sources and disposal points may vary according to the location of your home-site. If the site is within the limits of a municipality, there presumably will be water and sewer lines in the street in front of your property. If the site is in a new or remote subdivision, perhaps either you or the developer will have to pay the utilities to extend their facilities to reach your property. This must be ascertained when considering the purchase of a site, as such utility extensions can be damnably expensive if you are forced to pay for them. Here again, get any developer's promises in writing, so that you don't wind up holding a sewer or water line, rather than a bag.

With most municipal utilities, you are responsible for all piping on your property, with the utility owning all facilities up to and including any meters. So you have to get permission to tap any sewer or water lines, and must do, or have done, such taps in accordance to the regulations of the utility. A good many utilities will

demand that a licensed plumber perform all such connections. Check into all of these considerations before you complete planning, as perforce you are obliged to accede to the demands of regulatory authority. The plumbing may be one item which you might wish to contract, if you do not feel that you can build it well enough yourself. If you do contract it, the miserable bit of obtaining permits, buying materials of approved type, and conforming to all the whims of the bureaucracy, lies squarely upon the sagging shoulders of the plumbing contractor.

If your home-site is outside the limits of municipal utility service areas, you then inherit a whole new series of problems. There will then be no water or sewer lines to hook up to, so that water supply and waste disposal both must be resolved within the limits of your property. These problems must be considered when obtaining your home-site, as there may not be enough water underlying the property to drill an adequate well, and the soil can also be impervious, so that a septic tank and leaching field will not be practical. These are separate problems, but may be related to other issues, so that the purchase of a home-site becomes a complex matter, wherein you must consider a full spectrum of needs and desires. However, we are expounding on plumbing in this section, and will now proceed to attempt to explain the piping and accessories required for water supply, consumption or uses, and waste disposal for your adobe home.

If a municipal or other water supply system is not available, you will have to drill a well, that is, if your property is underlain with an aquifer from which an adequate supply of potable water may be drawn. We will presume that you have already investigated that problem, by checking other wells in the vicinity, retaining a competent Hydrologist, or querying the State Engineer, or whatever they call the office in charge of water use or quality within your state. Also, in most states, you will need a permit to drill your well, which is generally pro forma for domestic water use. Almost certainly, you will have to go to contract for the well, as the average person neither has access to a drilling rig nor the technical knowledge necessary to obtain a good well. The well should be cased in metal pipe, packed with gravel, surged and developed, flow tested, and equipped with the proper submersible pump and piping. When the well is completed, you are not yet home free, as some type of pressure system is needed so that the water can flow to all points of use. This requires either a large storage tank, located at an elevation higher than the points of use, or a pneumatic pressure system, which can be at or near the wellhouse. Unless you possess expertise in this field, contract it.

Now that your well is complete, tested, and certified as potable, or fit for human consumption, by a public health agency, and the pressure system is installed, you are at last up to the same point as if you were about to connect to a public water supply system. So, at this point, we shall digress a bit, and insert a list defining terms used in plumbing.

An Air Chamber is a short vertical section of pipe installed in a branch ahead of a faucet, which provides a space for air compression to cushion the shock when the flow of water is abruptly shut off.

A Branch is any secondary water or waste pipe which serves only one fixture.

A Cleanout Plug is a sewer fitting with a screwed plug, located at major bends in sewer lines, so that the plug may be removed to rod or unplug clogged drain lines.

A Closet Flange is a fitting attached to a toilet, so that the drain pipe may be connected.

A House Drain is the main sewer drain pipe, which collects the flow from all sewer branches, and runs to a point five feet outside the home's foundation wall.

A House Sewer is the piping that runs between the end of the house drain and the septic tank or public sewer line.

A Main is any major pipe to which branches are attached.

Plumbing is a generic term covering all pipes and fixtures used for the flow of water or wastewater.

A Riser is a vertical water supply line which extends upward at least one story.

"Roughing In" is the term used for the installation of all of the plumbing system, except for fixtures. This includes all piping, vents, or fixture supports.

A Septic Tank is a large water-tight covered tank, usually concrete, which receives the flow of wastewater from the house sewer line, converts it to a harmless liquid by bacterial action, and then permits it to flow into the open joint drain tile in the leaching field.

Soil Pipe is any line through which toilet sewage flows.

A Stack is a vertical main, soil, waste or vent pipe.

A Trap is a segment of curved pipe which, holding water through the bottom of its arc at all times, prevents the escape of sewer gases, while permitting the free flow of wastewater.

A Vent is a vertical pipe leading to atmosphere to supply air to permit free flow in drain lines.

A Waste pipe is one that carries other than toilet sewage.

Wastewater is a generic term for all used water, such as the drainage from sinks, lavatories, toilets, washers, tubs, showers or other points of water use.

The home's service line, leading from the well or utility's water main, may be from three-quarter

PLUMBING

TYPICAL PIPING LAYOUT

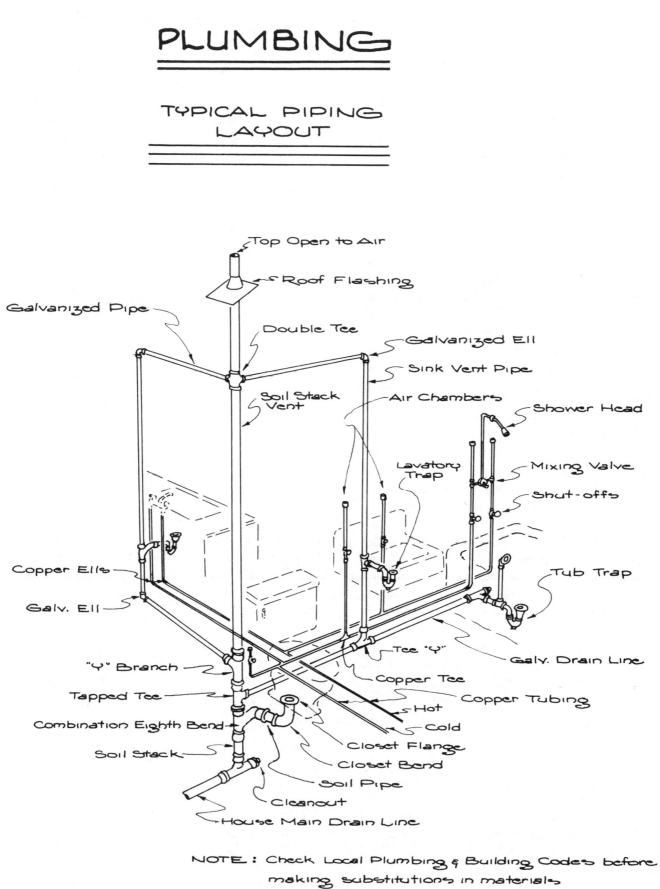

Top Open to Air

Roof Flashing

Galvanized Pipe

Double Tee

Galvanized Ell

Sink Vent Pipe

Soil Stack Vent

Air Chambers

Shower Head

Lavatory Trap

Mixing Valve

Shut-offs

Copper Ells

Galv. Ell

Tub Trap

"Y" Branch

Tee "Y"

Galv. Drain Line

Tapped Tee

Copper Tee

Combination Eighth Bend

Copper Tubing

Hot

Cold

Soil Stack

Closet Flange

Closet Bend

Soil Pipe

Cleanout

House Main Drain Line

NOTE: Check Local Plumbing & Building Codes before making substitutions in materials or methods.

to one inch or more in inside diameter, depending upon the number of residents, and the extent of water-use facilities, such as automatic washers, dishwashers, lawn sprinklers, etc. The home's water service main is laid as a spine, from which the branches lead to the various fixtures or appliances. It is best to locate valves at each branch, and in selected critical locations along the main, so that work can be done on segments of the system without shutting off all water to the home. Plan the location of the main with considerable thought and detail, so that branches are not too long, and to provide capacity and accessibility for any future additions. Each bathroom will require branches for lavatories, tub or shower, and the toilet. These may be from ⅜″ to ½″ inside diameter, depending upon fixture or Code demands. Air chambers should be installed on all branches just ahead of the faucet or unit. The branches for the kitchen may include sinks, refrigerators with icemakers, clothes washers, or dishwashers. You may even wish a branch into a living room, study or den to serve a wet bar. A major branch will be needed to serve the hot water heater, and don't forget outside outlets for hoses, patio service, lawn sprinklers and the like.

A main will also lead from the hot water heater to serve branches to all hot water faucets, tubs or shower, and wherever else you may need hot water. Don't forget that the hot water heater has to be able to function, and will require either an electric circuit or a gas line, or both, to serve it. If you use natural gas, there is yet another piping system to be built. Again, contact the gas utility company to determine their requirements, as they have a legal right to refuse to provide gas service to any facility they consider to be unsafe.

Your home's wastewater system begins at the drain of each fixture or water-using appliance, all of which must have traps installed at the drain-point. Waste lines will have to be of larger pipe size than water lines, as the water lines are under pressure, and the waste lines flow by gravity, and therefore require more pipe area for the slower flows. Each and every waste

line must slope in the direction of flow, by at least one-quarter inch per foot. Do not, repeat, do not, permit any drain line to be laid flat, or god forbid, with reversed slope. If you do this, that segment of line will be a trouble spot from the day you lay it, until the day you finally tear it out and replace it. Checking for proper slope in a drain line is not hard, and should be done on the entire length of every single run of pipe, that is, with the exception of vertical stacks, as you may assume that a vertical pipe will permit flow by gravity.

One very easy method for checking the slope of drain lines is with a carpenter's level and a small block of wood. The wood is attached to the bottom of one end of the level, and is as thick as the minimum slope for the length of the level; i.e., given a ¼″/ft. minimum slope and a level that is 36″ long, the wood block should be ¾″ thick. To check the slope, place the level on top of the pipe with the wood block in the direction of flow. If the level's bubble is toward the end with the block, the slope is too flat, and must be changed. If the bubble is centered, the slope is exactly at minimum, and if the bubble is toward the end of the level away from the wood block, the slope of the pipe exceeds minimum, and you're okay. Check each piece of pipe for adequate slope, but don't waste your time trying to check over joints, as the slope changes right at the joint, if at all.

Waste lines carrying only used water, with no solid wastes or sewage, should be at least two inches inside diameter for branches, and at least four inches for mains. Soil pipes carrying sewage should be four inch minimum. All mains should be four inch minimum, or six inch for very large families. A two to four inch vertical vent must be located near each fixture, but may be joined to other vents for a four inch stack projecting through the roof by at least two feet. The illustration in this section shows an example of typical plumbing layout, which you revise to suit your own needs.

The piping for all of your plumbing has to

SEWAGE DISPOSAL

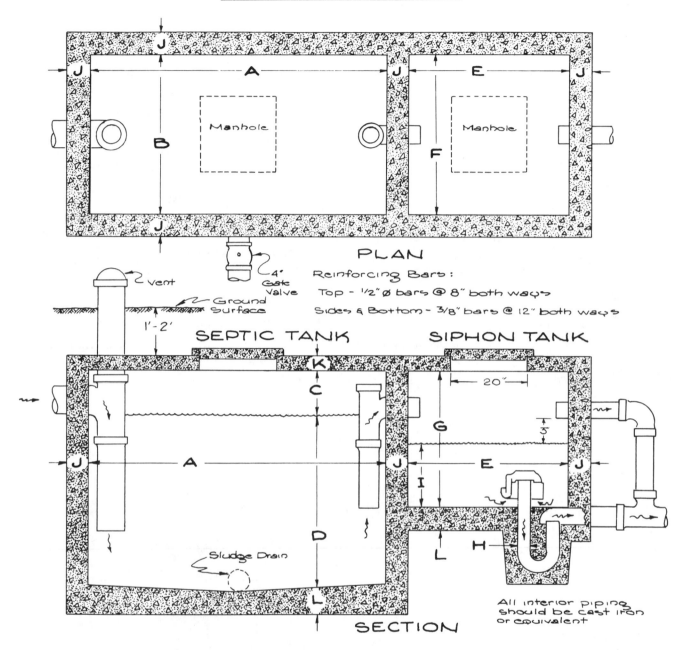

PLAN

Reinforcing Bars:

Top - 1/2" ⌀ bars @ 8" both ways

Sides & Bottom - 3/8" bars @ 12" both ways

SEPTIC TANK   SIPHON TANK

SECTION

All interior piping should be cast iron or equivalent

NO. IN HOME	SEPTIC TANK					SIPHON TANK					CONCRETE		
	CAP. GALS.	A	B	C	D	E	F	G	H	I	J	K	L
1-4	450	6'-0"	2'-6"	1'-0"	4'-0"	3'-0"	2'-6"	3'-0"	3"	1'-6"	6"	4"	6"
5-7	720	7'-0"	3'-6"	1'-0"	4'-0"	3'-6"	3'-6"	3'-0"	3"	1'-6"	6"	4"	6"
8-10	1000	8'-0"	4'-0"	1'-0"	4'-0"	4'-0"	4'-0"	3'-0"	4"	1'-8"	6"	4"	6"
11-12	1250	9'-0"	4'-6"	1'-0"	4'-3"	4'-6"	4'-6"	3'-0"	4"	1'-8"	7"	5"	6"
13-15	1480	9'-6"	4'-8"	1'-3"	4'-6"	4'-8"	4'-8"	3'-6"	4"	2'-2"	8"	5"	6"
15-17	1720	10'-0"	5'-0"	1'-3"	4'-8"	5'-0"	5'-0"	3'-6"	4"	2'-2"	8"	5"	6"
18-20	1950	10'-6"	5'-3"	1'-3"	4'-9"	5'-3"	5'-3"	3'-6"	4"	2'-2"	9"	5"	6"

go inside walls, under floors, and through foundation walls, and must be well planned. The vertical alignment of water lines is not critical, if the pipe is laid in as straight lines as you can manage. The vertical alignment of waste lines is quite critical, so resolve any pipe or duct conflict in favor of the waste line.

The house sewer line will lead either into a public sewer line, or into a septic tank. The drawing shows a typical septic tank, and a table of required sizes based on home population. When sizing your septic tank, use the size for the maximum probable residency in your home, not the present total. The discharge end of the septic tank is fitted with 4″ open-joint drain tile, which is from one hundred to one thousand feet in length, depending upon the home's residency and the permeability of the soil in the leaching field. Do not permit the septic tank or drain tile to flow toward your well, keep them over one hundred feet apart, and drain everything away from the well site.

There are several varieties of pipe material for plumbing use, any of which have their assets and liabilities. Copper tubing is now the best and easiest for either hot or cold water supply, although some of the plastics, such as polyvinyl chloride, or PVC, are offering stiff competition where its use is permitted by building codes. Cast iron is considered superior for all waste lines, although again plastic is challenging where permitted. To save money, stack vents may be steel pipe and the house sewer outside the foundation may be vitrified clay. There are other types of pipe on the market for each use, but you will have to investigate whether the local building codes will permit their use.

In this section, we won't even consider the myriad of fixtures available, as this can get into interior decorating and room planning.

CHAPTER XII

Financing Your Adobe Home

In common with the rest of us poor mortals, you will probably have to borrow at least some of the money needed to complete your adobe home, as if you had enough cash, you'd presumably ignore this book, and retain both an architect and a contractor.

The detailed planning for your adobe home must include financial considerations, as you will encounter cash expenditures of varying magnitude at intervals throughout the span of the project. The first big money need may be the funds to purchase the home-site, then, perhaps there are one or more aspects of the detailed plans for the home where you may decide that you need professional help, so there might be a fee for an architect or engineer. Even if you make your own adobe blocks, some construction materials must be purchased, such as lumber, perhaps ready-mix concrete, window and door units, pipe, wiring, wallboard and on and on and on. If you need a well, there is a well-drilling contractor, and perhaps the assistance of a plumber or electrician, and you may decide to hire some labor to speed up the project. The furnace and all of the many fixtures and appliances will burn up cash, as will all of the continuing expenses of daily life, plus whatever mortgage, loan or time payment obligations that are undertaken to secure funds to complete your home.

During all of your detailed planning, you will make numerous decisions on how, what, when, where and why you will do certain things to accomplish specific results, and you must also

consider how you are going to pay for the items needed to attain these results. Thus, if you lay out a program of the work necessary to complete your home in an orderly schedule, you will also have an approximation of your cash flow needs. That is, when you have decided on the order of work, what items you may contract, and all of the materials to purchase, you will be able to estimate the amount of money that you must expend during a given period of time. This may require some severe budgeting on your part, as you can delay the project significantly if you have to wait to obtain funds to pay for services or products that may be pivotal points which prevent further progress without their completion.

Once you have established your cash flow needs, as approximately when and how much, you can start to investigate fund sources. Perhaps the best source of these funds may be your own savings over some few years. The average person will need several years or more to bring his adobe home from dream to completed, being-lived-in reality. Most folks have some kind of saving program, which can be accelerated or enlarged during the dreaming, wishing and actual planning stages. If you don't have a savings program, the time to start it was yesterday, as your own money doesn't cost you a cent in interest or carrying charges. If you really bear down to scrimp and save, you may be pleasantly surprised at how much you can set aside while you are planning your adobe home. As we have continually insisted, adequate planning for this project is going to take a considerable period of time, for if it doesn't, you simply have not done a satisfactory job of work.

Good, detailed planning can also be an asset in obtaining funds with which to complete the project. For, if you walk into a lender's office, loudly announce that you want to build a house, and ask how much money he will loan you, you may be given only specific directions on how to get out of his office. Whereas, if you went to that same lender and showed him a detailed set of home plans and an estimated cash flow schedule, you may very well walk out of there with a check in your hot little hand.

The acquisition of your home-site will be one of the earliest and perhaps largest of the necessary expenditures, if you do not already own that property. As we have said before, the home-site should be obtained as early as possible, as the site will affect both the home's design and your total cash outlay. Also, paid-off, or even partially encumbered property may be accepted as security for a construction loan. The price of land seems to spiral ever upward, so that if you should come across a prospective home-site that meets all of your needs and desires, buy it now, even if you don't plan to start your adobe home project for some time.

Once you have established an estimated cash flow schedule, you will have determined how much of the need may be met with your own resources, and how much and approximately when, will have to be borrowed. Don't wait right up to the day you will need the borrowed funds, but investigate the loan possibilities and probable cost as soon as you have isolated the need. The source of the funds may, in some degree, depend on the size of the need. If the specific need is a periodic outlay for lumber, fittings, etc., then check into the credit policies of the local building supply firms. These businesses may be used to dealing with do-it-yourselfers, and may perhaps offer a line of credit, with monthly payments tailored to your budget. If the need is a large amount, such as capital outlays for furnaces,

appliances or contractors fees, then a bank or savings and loan may be the best source. Perhaps you may wish to borrow at once the entire amount that will be needed, over and above your own resources, to complete all of the project so as to take advantage of price reductions for volume purchases.

Don't be afraid to check around for the lowest interest rates on these loans, so that you get the best obtainable deal at the least cost to you. If you have decided to go the contract route for all or most of your home, you will presumably have to finance that cost with a long-term mortgage. If you feel that you either can't or don't want to do all of that hard work yourself, contract is the only solution, so go to it. A long-term mortgage may be hard to get for a self-built home, as the mortgagor may have justified doubts about the completed value of the project, or indeed, whether or not it will ever be completed. Such loans are often made on evaluation of the borrower, as well as the project to be financed. Loan officers frequently give more consideration to reputation of the prospective borrower, his credit record and personal reliability, than they do to the merits of the project itself.

Some other possible fund sources may involve loans on your life insurance, friends and relatives, private investors, and as a last resort, the high-interest short-term loan companies.

Your financing will be a highly individual matter, as the actual cash flow demand will be affected by everything that touches upon the project, from the scope of your plans, the extent of the work that you intend to do yourself, down to the anticipated time for completion. Try to be as flexible in the planning of financial commitments as possible. Remember that the unexpected almost invariably occurs, so don't get so tied up in payments that there is no reserve for contingencies or emergencies. Also, the longer the term of the mortgage or loan, the more it is going to cost in interest, so try to get early payback provisions included in the financing, in order to avoid paying interest for the full term of a note, if you can manage to pay back earlier.

Detailed planning can aid to resolve problems as they arise, rather than causing undue delays to eliminate the difficulty. This project is going to take a very long time to accomplish with good planning, and even longer with poor work. When you consider that you might live in this adobe home for the rest of your life, the amount of time consumed in adequate planning fades into insignificance, when even remotely compared to the benefits to be derived.

If as much as possible of the work is done with your own hands, the end result will be a better home than you otherwise could have afforded, as you can expend more funds for materials, fixtures, appliances, and little frills and comforts, than if you had to pay through the nose for all of that labor. Don't forget to include at least some of the frills and luxuries, as a very spartan home can in time become very irritating. Which all leads back into our basic premise, plan, plan, and yet again, plan.

CHAPTER XIII

The Adobe Home — Typical Floor Plans

This chapter will set forth a dozen alternate floor plan conceptions for your Adobe Home. You will find that these are not detailed designs, but concepts of layouts offered only to stimulate your own ideas. These offerings have been limited to single-floor two or three bedroom layouts, in both Territorial and Pueblo styles. This is not to indicate that Adobe Homes should be limited to this scope, indeed not, but simply to keep the size of this book within bounds while attempting to satisfy the requirements of the majority.

An Adobe Home may be anything that you wish it to be, large and imposing, small and comfortable, traditional or modern. The difference between Territorial and Pueblo stylings is not structurally significant, depending to a large extent upon the variation of trims and materials. So the choice is completely up to you, as these offerings have been set forth to aid, not to limit, your own planning. These floor plans have purposely been kept comparatively simple, so that some variation or combination of these offerings would satisfy the needs of the majority. You, who will live in this Adobe Home, must satisfy your own needs and desires. Consider these offerings, study your own wishes, perhaps consulting an architect, engineer or contractor.

FLOOR PLAN NO. 1

This is a simple two-bedroom Pueblo style with approximately 1,200 square feet of living space. This particular layout is also quite adaptable to Territorial styling by the addition of brick copings, the squaring-off of the arched portal columns, etc.

This layout would be very livable for a small family, compact, accessible, with possibilities for later expansion. Depending upon the size and configuration of the site chosen, a patio may be placed at the back of the house, or along one or both sides of the portal.

The portal surrounding two sides of the house provides ample space for shade, recreation or just plain loafing. This plan, if built offset toward the left rear of a lot, offers room for landscaping as desired, either simple or complex, centered upon the portal.

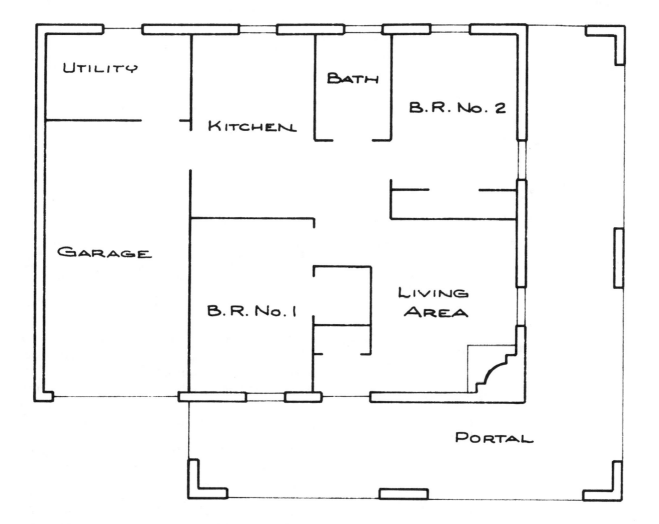

UTILITY

BATH

B.R. No. 2

KITCHEN

GARAGE

B.R. No. 1

LIVING AREA

PORTAL

Scale: 1/10" to 1'

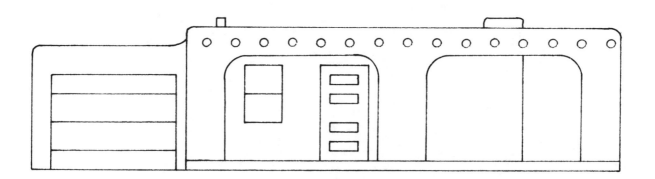

FLOOR PLAN NO. 1

FLOOR PLAN NO. 2

Here is a two-bedroom Territorial home, of approximately 1,400 square feet of living space. This basic layout can be extensively varied to suit different needs. The central partition formed from the fireplace and closets is inherently adaptable to fulfill individual requirements.

As with Floor Plan No. 1, the plumbing is simplified by the longitudinal grouping of kitchen, utility and bath.

A patio stretching from the walled garden along the back of the house would be attractive and accessible. This home could be quite attractively landscaped if located somewhat to the right rear of the chosen site.

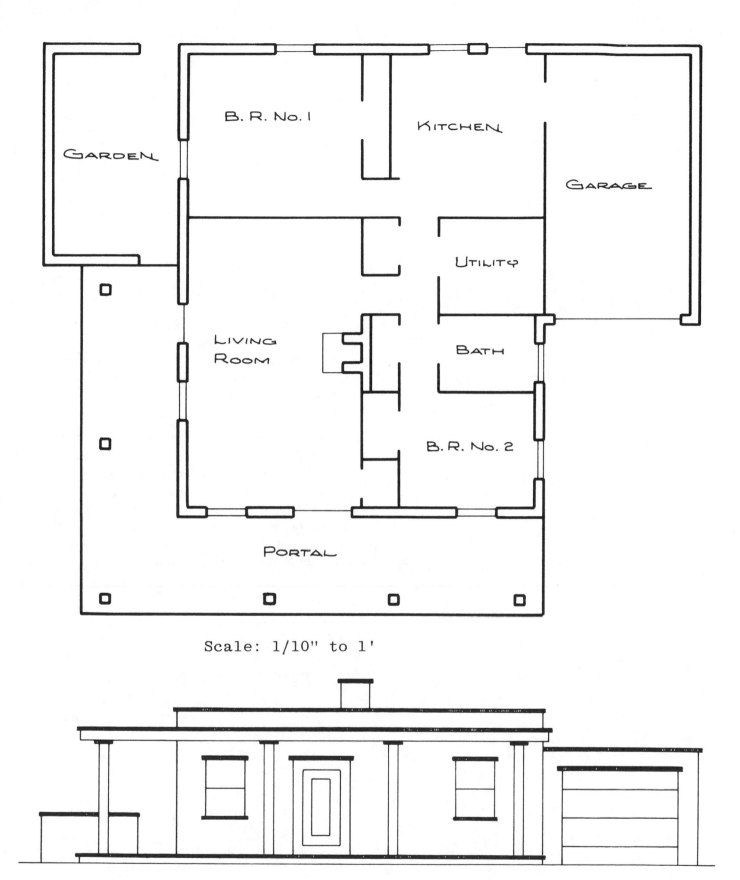

GARDEN

B. R. No. 1

KITCHEN

GARAGE

UTILITY

LIVING ROOM

BATH

B. R. No. 2

PORTAL

Scale: 1/10" to 1'

FLOOR PLAN NO. 2

FLOOR PLAN NO. 3

This Pueblo-style two bedroom home has approximately 1,700 square feet of living space, including two baths and a den. The layout offers many opportunities for revision, and would be quite suitable for a small, but perhaps growing family.

The partition between the kitchen and the living area would be built of adobe bricks, unplastered but whitewashed or painted. The brick texture provides pleasing contrast for both rooms. The L-shaped living area affords interesting decoration and use possibilities, and the window indicated adjacent to the kitchen could be a large picture window with a vista of a landscaped area, or could be changed to sliding or french doors leading onto a patio.

This layout does not show a garage, which could be built as a separate structure, perhaps with shop facilities, or as a carport attached to either the rear or side of the kitchen.

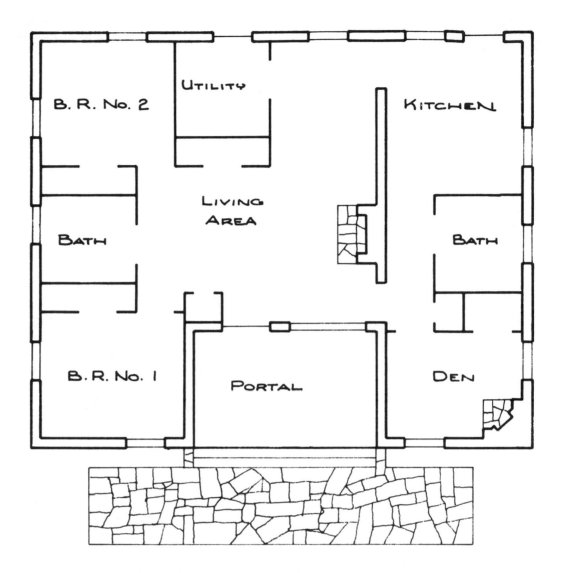

Scale: 1/10" to 1'

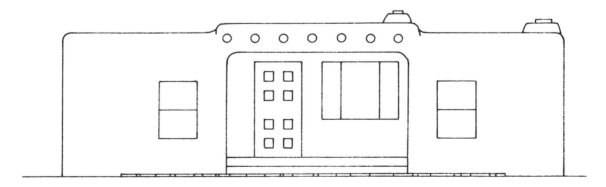

FLOOR PLAN NO. 3

FLOOR PLAN NO. 4

This floor plan shows a Territorial two-bedroom home with an approximate 1,400 square feet living area, but which appears larger because of the linear arrangement.

Here again, use could be made of adobe brick for one or more of the interior partitions, such as the one between the living area and the master bedroom. The large corner fireplace offers the opportunity for varied treatment in decoration, perhaps wood paneling or wainscoting. The fairly short portal may be extended around the side of the house, or relieved by flower beds or shrubs.

This layout is adaptable to a large variety of siting, but should be located to obtain maximum benefit of views from the living area windows.

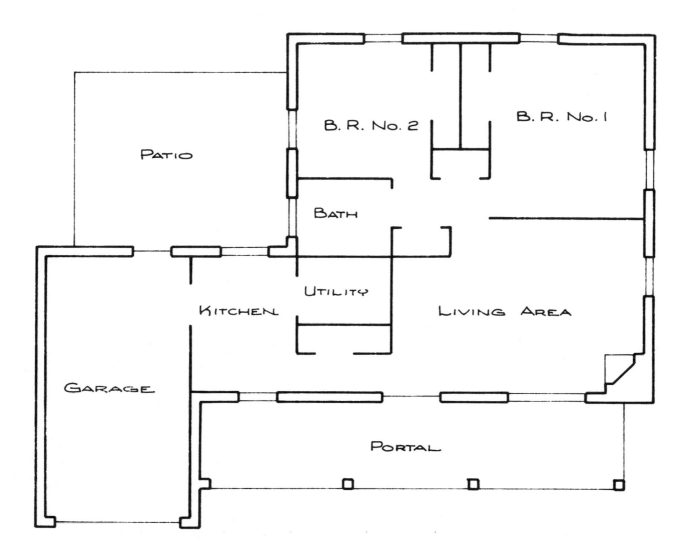

Patio

B. R. No. 2

B. R. No. 1

Bath

Utility

Kitchen

Living Area

Garage

Portal

Scale: 1/10" to 1'

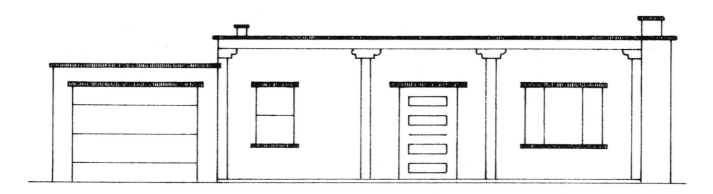

FLOOR PLAN NO. 4

FLOOR PLAN NO. 5

This Pueblo-style two-bedroom, containing approximately 1,500 square feet of living area, is almost wrapped around the semi-enclosed patio, affording maximum privacy for crowded locations.

The entire fireplace wall in the living area, from the patio across the kitchen, could be completely adobe block, both for loadbearing and decoration. The waist-high wall on the portal provides an excellent background for flower beds, as well as increased weather protection.

This layout would fit well on a small city lot, with a low adobe wall around the property line, both for decoration and privacy.

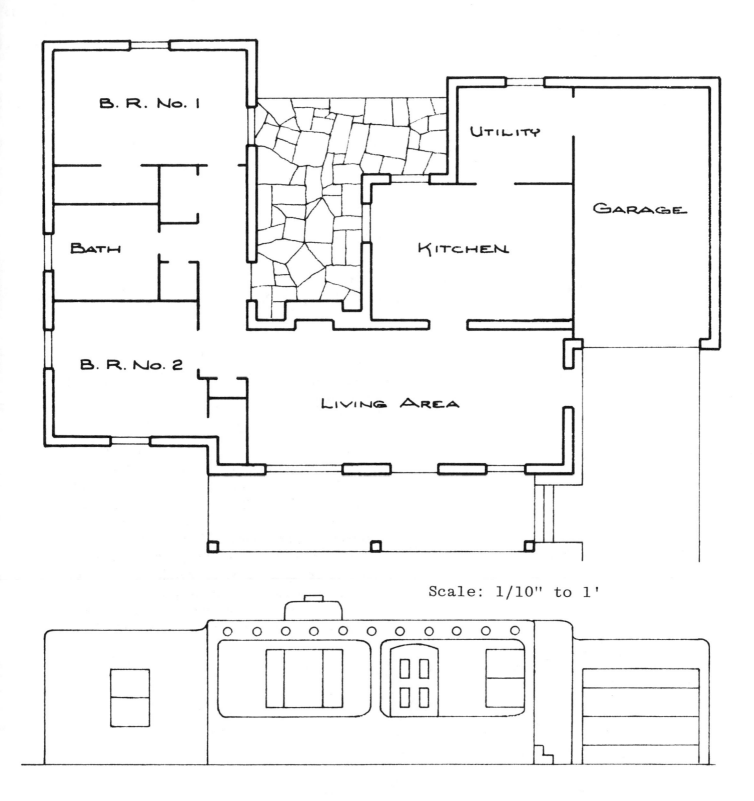

B. R. No. 1

Utility

Garage

Bath

Kitchen

B. R. No. 2

Living Area

Scale: 1/10" to 1'

FLOOR PLAN NO. 5

FLOOR PLAN NO. 6

This attractive two-bedroom Territorial home contains approximately 2,200 square feet of living area, including the completely enclosed interior patio.

This layout is quite adaptable for the growing family, or for any other variable needs. The fireplace, with stub adobe walls on each side, forms an effective room divider between the living room and kitchen, while still leaving ample room for passage-ways. The interior patio may be left open to the sky, or may be covered with transparent or translucent glass or plastic for weather protection. The garage may be doubled to two or more car size, providing a sheltered angle for an exterior patio or garden.

The large two-sided portal makes an open background for flower beds or other landscaping.

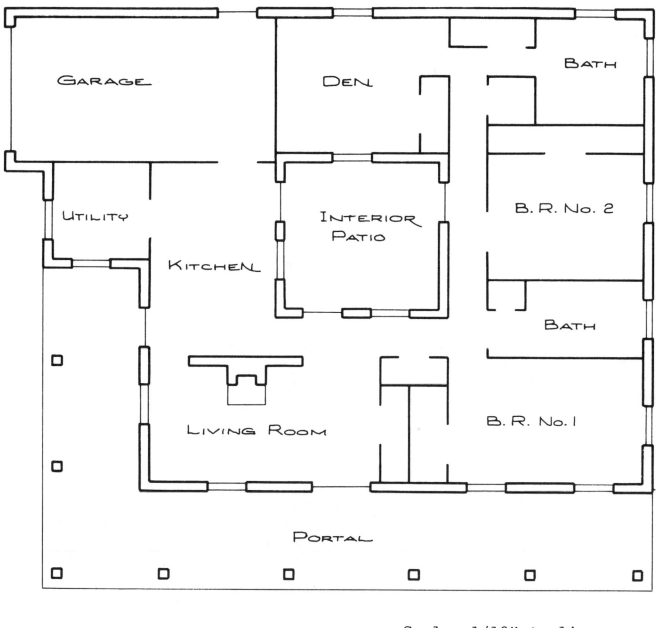

GARAGE

DEN

BATH

UTILITY

INTERIOR PATIO

B. R. No. 2

KITCHEN

LIVING ROOM

BATH

B. R. No. 1

PORTAL

Scale: 1/10" to 1'

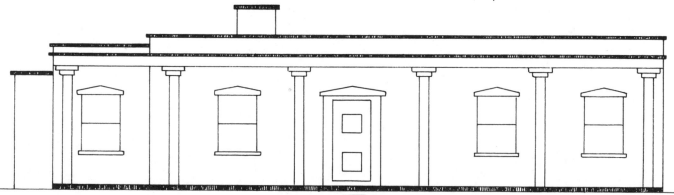

FLOOR PLAN NO. 6

FLOOR PLAN NO. 7

Here is a Pueblo-style two-bedroom home of approximately 1,400 square feet living space, with a flagstone patio around three sides of the living area.

This layout lends itself to almost infinite possibilities in decoration, with only a stub adobe wall dividing the entry, kitchen and living area. This plan would also be adaptable to Territorial styling, as a three-sided covered portal could replace the open patio. This home is quite suitable for a large variety of site locations and sizes.

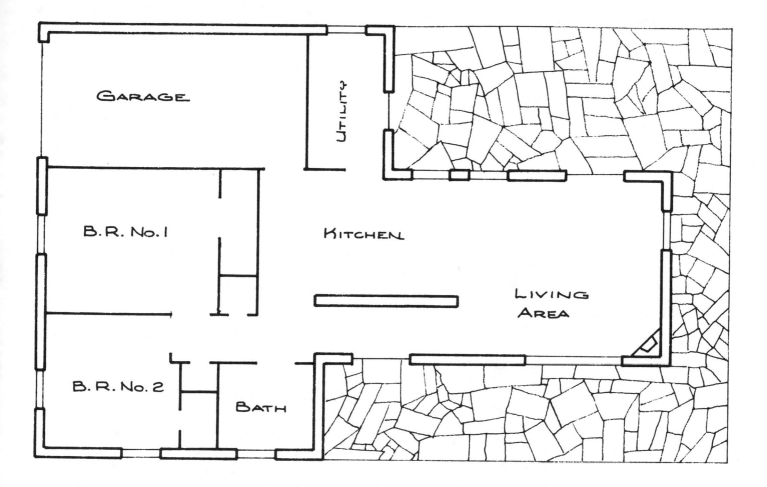

GARAGE

UTILITY

B.R. No.1

KITCHEN

LIVING AREA

B.R. No.2

BATH

Scale: 1/10" to 1'

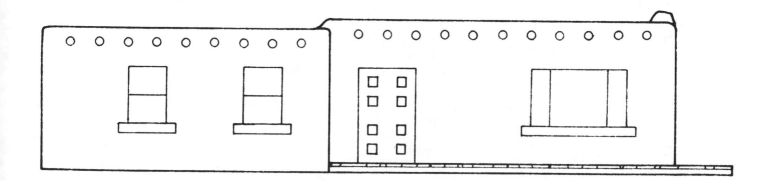

FLOOR PLAN NO. 7

FLOOR PLAN NO. 8

This Territorial-style three-bedroom home contains almost 1,800 square feet of living space.

The L-shaped adobe interior wall supports the large fireplace, and creates an effective divider between the living room and kitchen, yet leaves enough open space for livability. The low-walled patio leading from the portal to the rear of the house provides areas for both recreation and miniature landscaping. This layout is adaptable to either a corner city lot or a large tract.

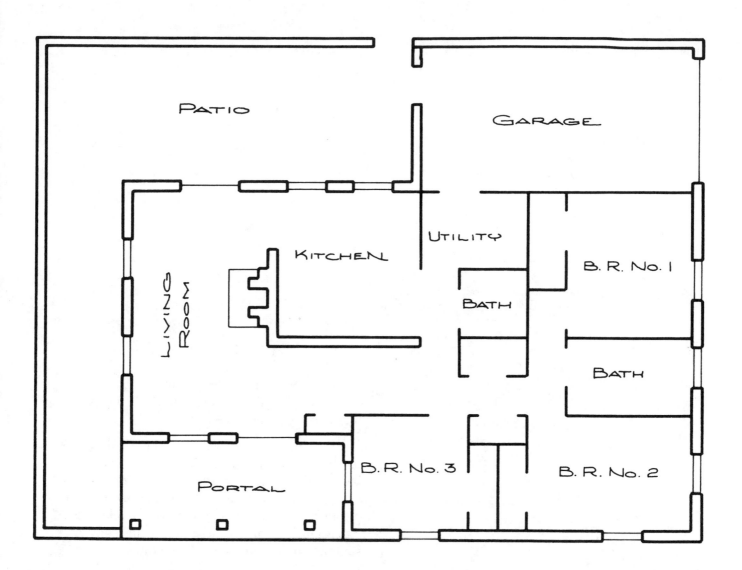

Patio

Garage

Kitchen

Utility

Living Room

B. R. No. 1

Bath

Bath

Portal

B. R. No. 3

B. R. No. 2

Scale: 1/10" to 1'

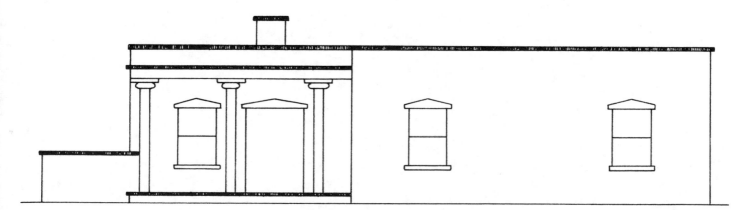

FLOOR PLAN NO. 8

FLOOR PLAN NO. 9

The 1,900 square feet of living space in this three-bedroom Pueblo-style home includes two baths and a study or den.

The load-bearing wall on the right of the living area supports the fireplace, creates the back hall, and affords room for closets, built-in cabinets, or other use. Note that there is no partition or barrier between the kitchen and living area, leaving a large area with many possibilities for varied use and decoration.

If the selected site is large enough, this plan would be enhanced by a large walled garden, either along the rear or surrounding the entire house.

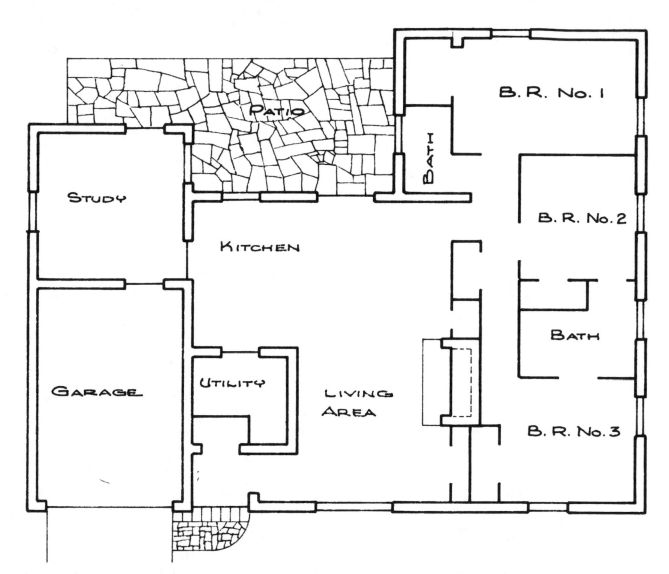

Scale: 1/10" to 1'

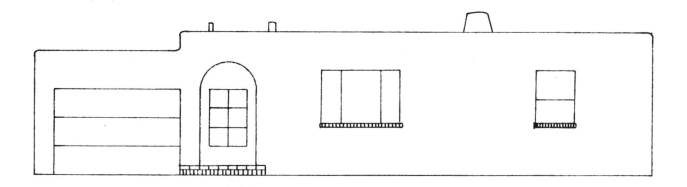

FLOOR PLAN NO. 9

FLOOR PLAN NO. 10

This Territorial three-bedroom home could be quite imposing, containing over 1,600 square feet of living space, but appearing much larger.

The low wall encompassing three sides of the home may be built near the lot line, or on a larger site, used to accentuate more extensive landscaping.

The fireplace, half enclosed by an adobe stub wall, creates an entryway, and also acts as a focal point for the living room. This plan affords a maximum of living space in a compact, readily built layout.

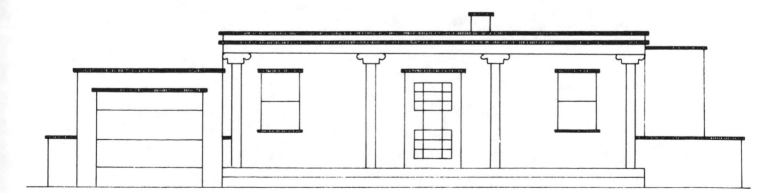

GARDEN

B. R. No. 1

BATH

B. R. No. 3

BATH

B. R. No. 2

UTILITY

LIVING
ROOM

KITCHEN

PATIO

GARAGE

PORTAL

Scale: 1/10" to 1'

FLOOR PLAN NO. 10

FLOOR PLAN NO. 11

This plan shows a Pueblo-style home with over 2,000 square feet of livability, either three bedrooms or two bedrooms and study.

This house should be built with extensive use of whitewashed or painted adobe interior walls, including the wall on the left of the living area and the divider between the kitchen and living area. The setting of the fireplace outside the line of the front wall gives a vigorous front effect with the large chimney structure, and also leaves more usable space in the living area.

The wall at the rear of the enclosed patio should be house-high, affording maximum privacy. Low adobe or rock walls may be built around the inside perimeter of the enclosure, forming planter boxes, seats or storage space. A tiny fountain in the center of this patio would not be amiss.

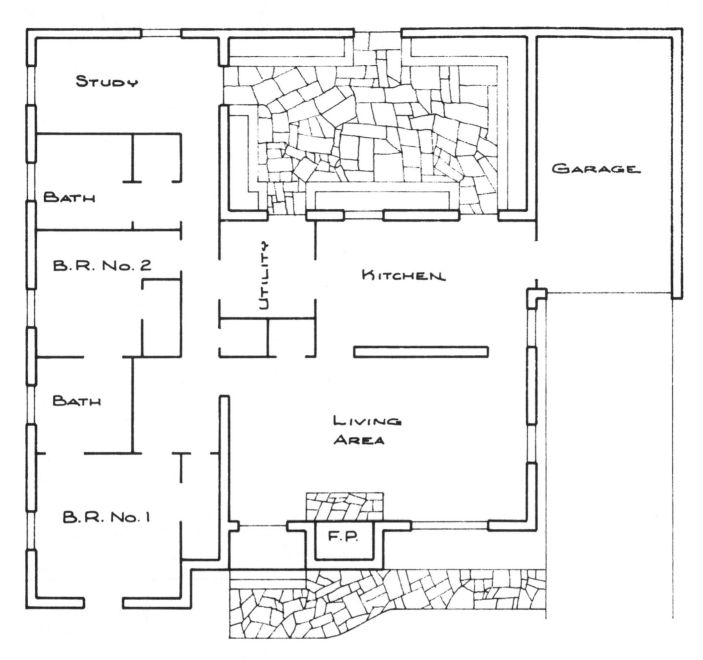

STUDY

BATH

B.R. No. 2

BATH

B.R. No. 1

UTILITY

KITCHEN

GARAGE

LIVING
AREA

F.P.

Scale: 1/10" to 1'

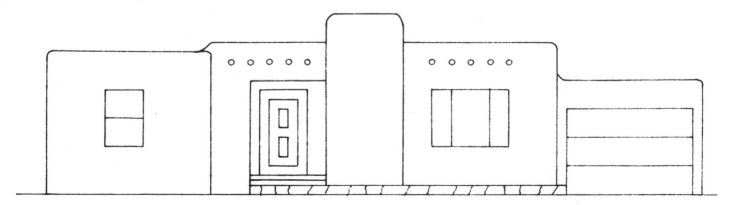

FLOOR PLAN NO. 11

FLOOR PLAN NO. 12

This last floor plan offering shows a three-bedroom Territorial with over 2,200 square feet of living space.

The T-shaped raised portal creates an almost Baronial effect, while the front-to-back living area may be used as one large space, or divided by hangings, screens or other temporary barriers into living and dining areas. The interior adobe or rock stub wall enhances the fireplace, creates the hallway and sets off the kitchen from the living area.

Placed upon a moderate to large-sized lot, this home would be set off by a low adobe wall, topped by Territorial brick coping, around the lot line. This layout almost demands semi-formal Southwestern landscaping.

These floor plans have been offered as suggestions to stimulate your own ideas. So examine your needs, try to fulfill your desires, consider all alternatives.

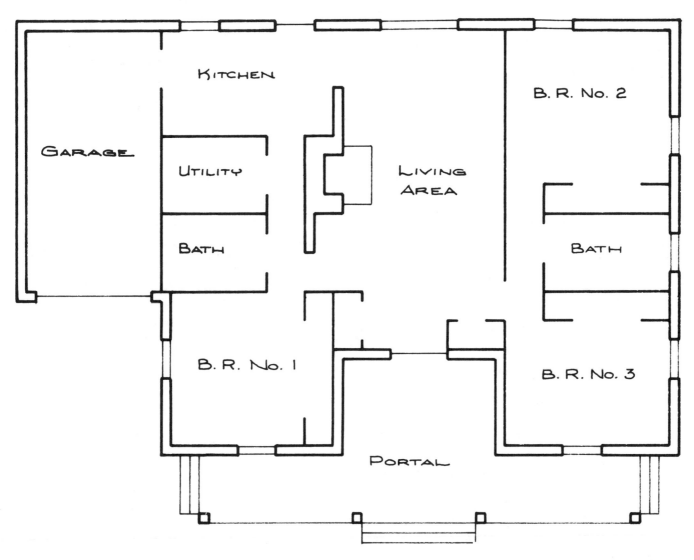

GARAGE

KITCHEN

UTILITY

BATH

LIVING AREA

B. R. No. 2

BATH

B. R. No. 1

B. R. No. 3

PORTAL

Scale: 1/10" to 1'

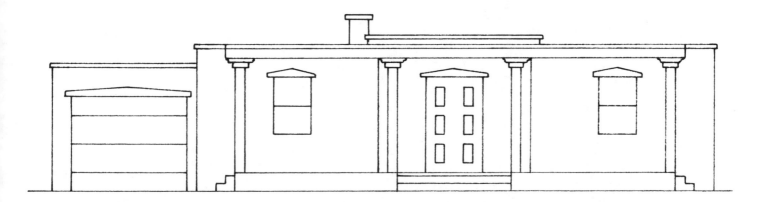

FLOOR PLAN NO. 12

CHAPTER XIV

The Interior Of Your Adobe Home

Up to now, we have been so immersed in all of the other aspects of your adobe home, that we have almost ignored the most important basic purpose of the project, the provision of adequate, attractive, comfortable living space.

A dozen home floor plans have been inserted in this book, but are offered only as suggestions to stimulate the flow of your own ideas. It is our firm belief that a home's essential objective is to be lived-in, rather than the ostentation of a grandiose showpiece, and that the layout and interior of a home need suit only those who live in it. All that any floor plan accomplishes is to divide and enclose space, so you must again determine the allocation of space that will attain the specific ends to fulfill your own unique needs and desires. For you are unique, and your goals will differ in some degree from those of your friends or neighbors, so that your home will become a reflection of yourself.

The emphasis to be given to any particular area of the home in the division of space will be slanted entirely to suit your present and future needs, so that lengthy planning is demanded to determine and economically resolve those needs. You will undoubtedly spend more time on the layout and interior planning of the home than any other single aspect, as this planning will most affect your daily life in that home. The interior decoration of a room or house may nowadays he changed almost at will, but its basic size and shape will get a bit rough to alter. So that you should decide upon basic layout before giving too much detailed attention to decoration,

although probable decoration will enter into many of those decisions. There are severe practical limitations to be considered in this layout, as space itself costs time and money to enclose, and all of the wiring, piping, ductwork and other support elements should be compact networks, so that the entire spectrum of construction requirements must be balanced against the desired ends.

Therefore, we shall again proceed to offer our comments on some of the criteria involved in the layout and decoration of rooms in the adobe home, and leave up to you the resolution of your needs.

The kitchen may demand more detailed planning than other rooms in your home, as it may have the highest intensity of use, and its various facilities will be more permanent in nature. The location of each fixture or appliance should be laid out with care, as it is a bit difficult to re-arrange sinks, stoves and the like once they are installed. The kitchen will be laid out around primary functional areas, which are refrigerator and food storage, cooking and serving, and the sink and cleaning area. The dining area, or a breakfast nook, may also be a part of the kitchen, or an alcove, rather than a separate room. The pages of typical kitchen layouts illustrate how these areas are often arranged to permit smooth, even flow of the work for meal preparations.

A kitchen should be a bright, cheerful room with a high lighting level, and as much storage

TYPICAL KITCHEN LAYOUTS

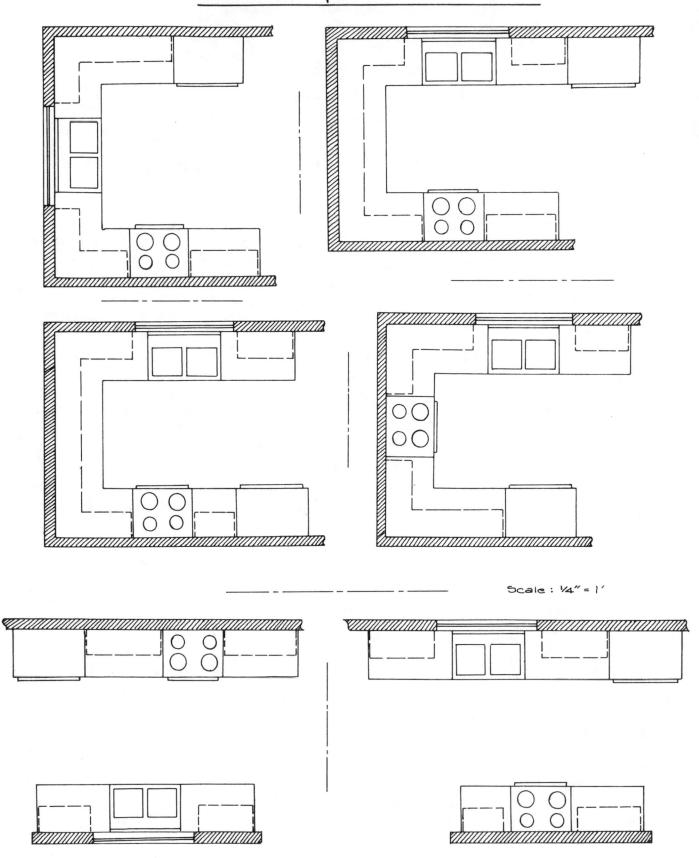

Scale : 1/4" = 1'

TYPICAL KITCHEN LAYOUTS

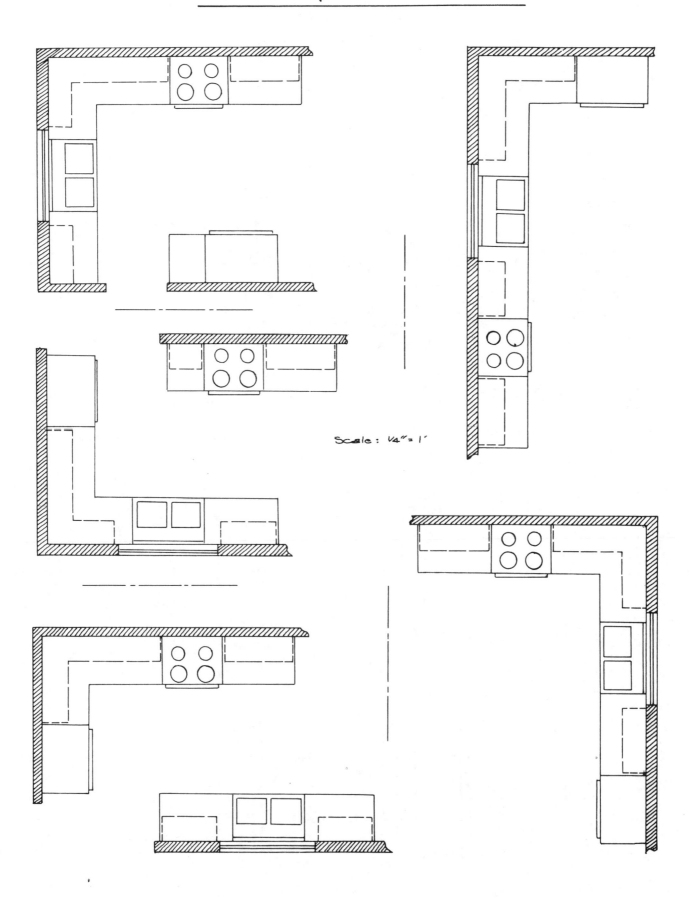

Scale: 1/4" = 1'

TYPICAL KITCHEN LAYOUTS

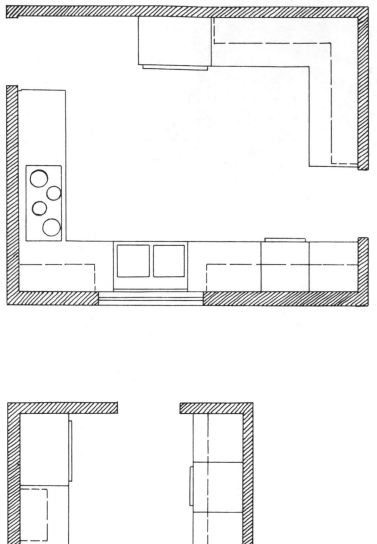

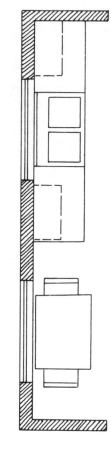

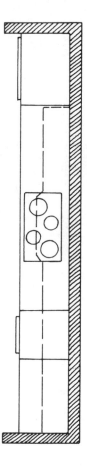

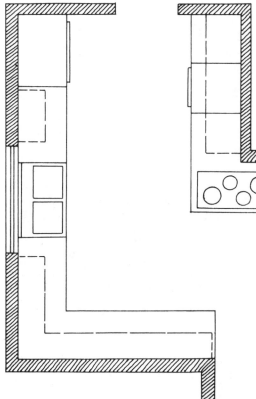

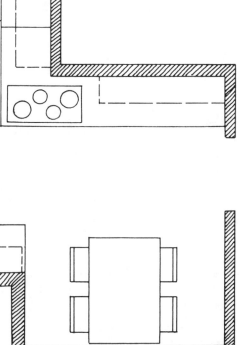

Various Room Shapes
demand Individual
Treatment. Use Your
imagination.

Scale: 1/4" = 1'

space as can be put into it. Some wives will insist that there is no such thing as too much kitchen storage. Cabinets above or below work areas and fixtures both supply storage, and offer opportunity for interesting decoration. Ready-made cabinets may be bought in units, or you can attempt to make your own, if you are good enough at woodworking. Cabinets with carved trim, inlaid doors, or carved bas-reliefs are very well suited to the decor of an adobe home, and do not have to be expensive custom-mades, as there are many veneer trims or glue-on appliques which can provide excellent results, if done with taste and good workmanship. Many of the ready-made cabinets are sized so that their installation, at reachable height from the floor by a woman, leaves a gap of one or two feet between the top of the cabinet and the ceiling. This space is an unattractive dustcatcher, and may be filled with a flush soffit from the cabinet top to the ceiling. This resolves the dustcatcher problem, could provide extra storage for rarely used items, and give you an opportunity to exercise ingenuity in selecting the soffit facade. The soffit can give cabinetry a built-in look, and may be of almost any material from painted wallboard, paneling to match the cabinet finish, Mexican tile for brightness, to any other material or fabric that will fit in the decorative scheme of the kitchen. A kitchen floor has to be a hard, durable, dense material to withstand the heavy traffic, and be easily cleaned. It can be anything from traditional brick to linoleum, or ceramic or vinyl tiles. If you haven't looked at linoleum floor coverings recently, you really should. There are more patterns and styles available than can be imagined, if you remember the drab product of bygone years, even to imitation brick or tile that has a very good appearance.

The counter tops and the limited wall area between the counters and cabinets may be covered with bright Mexican tile or vinyl, and the walls painted or paneled, or even wainscoted. The ceiling may be any type you prefer, from vigas and herringbone, conventional lath and plaster, gypsum or wallboard, to the newer suspended ceilings. The suspended ceiling offers a chance for flush-mounted lighting fixtures at less work than other types, but again, you have to choose what you want, the decor that best suits both your desires and by now sadly depleted checking account.

A bathroom does not have to be a drab, utilitarian space, but can be made very attractive at little or no more cost than strict utility. The bathrooms also deserve detailed planning, due in part to the piping and permanent installation of fixtures. Yes, we said bathrooms, plural not singular. If you need evidence of a rising standard of living, this could be it. We will always remember growing up in a rural home with five rooms and path, in a day when indoor plumbing in a rural home was a rare avis. Today, the great majority of new home construction, rural or urban, must have more than one bathroom. For a large family, two or more bathrooms have become grim necessity, particularly if there is more than one female in the home. Even for the couple with no children, two baths give a touch of comfort and luxury, and ease the stress and strain of getting ready for work, preparing for an evening out, or simple solitude and relaxation.

The illustrations of typical bathroom layouts offer examples of simple one-user-at-a-time rooms to large multi-use facilities. Again, they are included only as suggestions to stimulate your own ideas and solutions. When planning your bathrooms, provide more than enough area around fixtures to move around in, and base the dimensioning upon the exact fixtures you are going to use. There is a considerable variety of fixture sizes and styling on the market, so go out and check them to see what suits you best. Most men like a nice, large shower stall, with the shower head high enough so as not to have to stoop under it, while many women prefer a leisurely bath in a roomy tub, but whatever your family needs and wants, plan it and put it in. In many multiple bath installations, the rooms are located back-to-back to simplify the plumbing, and incidentally save some money. If this can be worked into your prospective floor plan, that's great. If you have some ideas or needs that

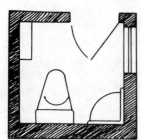

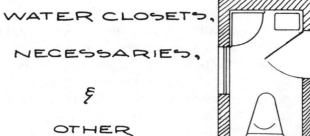

BATHROOMS,

POWDER ROOMS,

WATER CLOSETS,

NECESSARIES,

&

OTHER

SITES

FOR

WITHDRAWAL

&

SOLITUDE

——— · ———

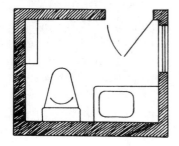

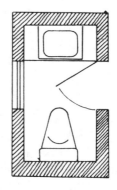

Scale : 1/4" = 1'

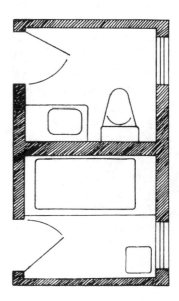

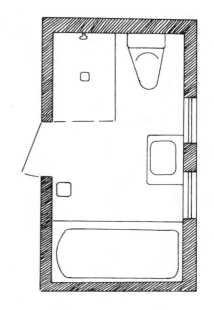

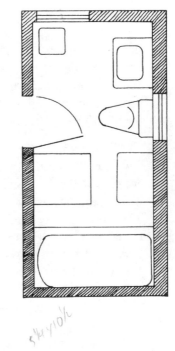

5'4" x 10½'

preclude this arrangement, it's no tragedy, but be prepared to spend more for plumbing.

Every bathroom must have some storage space, if only to hide the Lord of the Manor's razor and shaving gear. Towels and other bathing needs have to be stored somewhere and right at the point of use is ideal. Cabinets can be built into walls, over toilets and under lavatories. The bare lavatory sticking out of the wall is passé and inefficient, and should be enclosed, perhaps with a large counter-top or vanity in an alcove, with cabinet storage beneath. Again, your choice of materials is limited only by your taste and wallet. Cabinetry is available bare, for painting or staining, or in any type of finish or style that you can dream up. Bathroom floors may be tile, sheet vinyl or even carpeting in areas away from the tub or shower. The walls are often tiled, and varying patterns of Mexican tiles combined with standard white or pastel tiles may appeal to you.

One element of bathrooms that may often be inadequate or neglected is lighting. Shaving with a hangover by the light of one 40-watt bulb can be both enervating and painful. Various medicines are customarily kept in bathrooms, and selecting the wrong bottle in poor lighting can be fatal. Whether you choose fluorescents or incandescent bulbs, be sure to provide high-level lighting over or around the shaving or vanity mirrors, ceiling lighting, and enough outlets to serve your needs.

All corridors, halls or passageways must be wide enough to permit two adults to pass each other without one having to flatten against a wall. Closets and cabinets are convenient in such areas, if only to get more storage space without intruding upon living areas. Make all such areas wide enough so that another person can get past opened closet doors, etc. This is true of all traffic-flow zones in the home, so make all access wide enough to permit double passage without obstructions.

All adobe homes should have one or more fireplaces, and we mean real, functioning wood-burning fireplaces, not those benighted fakes with the jolly little plastic log and phony electric flames. A fireplace can be a very comforting thing on a cold, blustery winter's eve. It is not just the heat thrown out from it, but the whole aspect of the dancing flames, the scent of burning wood, and the brick or flagstone hearth that create an enormous appeal, perhaps historic, aesthetic or primitive, but satisfying.

Fireplaces can be put into almost any room, but may be most appropriate in den, study, master bedroom, and especially in the living room. They may be any style or size, from a tiny adobe beehive in a corner to a massive brick or stone affair that may span half a wall. The fireplace illustrations show differing styles, and also construction details. Any size fireplace may be built by adapting the dimensions in the table to the same proportions for the size that you desire. The facade of the fireplace can be trimmed with stone, brick, wood, tile or plastered or bare adobe blocks, to blend into the decor of the room. The hearth may be tiny or large, of brick or stone, perhaps trimmed or bordered with Mexican tile.

A bedroom should be more than just a place to sleep, and can be made large enough to hold bed, bureau, chest of drawers and perhaps a desk and chair, and one or more comfortable chairs without overcrowding. Adequate closet space is mandatory, and can be anything from a small bare minimum to large walk-ins, or even shelving and drawers built into the wall. The trim and decor of a bedroom depends upon the age and sex of the primary occupant, although one should not go overboard on the trim of little children's rooms, as those kids will grow up, and may not later appreciate being stuck with permanent fixtures of juvenile variety.

The living room or family room must above all be comfortable, rather than a stiff exhibition showpiece. It should be large and airy, and will be the most adaptable room in the home for revisions in decor and furniture arrangement. The fireplace may be in a corner, a major outside wall, or even very effectively against a short segment of adobe wall acting as a room divider.

SOME
TYPICAL
FIREPLACES
IN
ADOBE HOMES

TYPICAL FIREPLACES

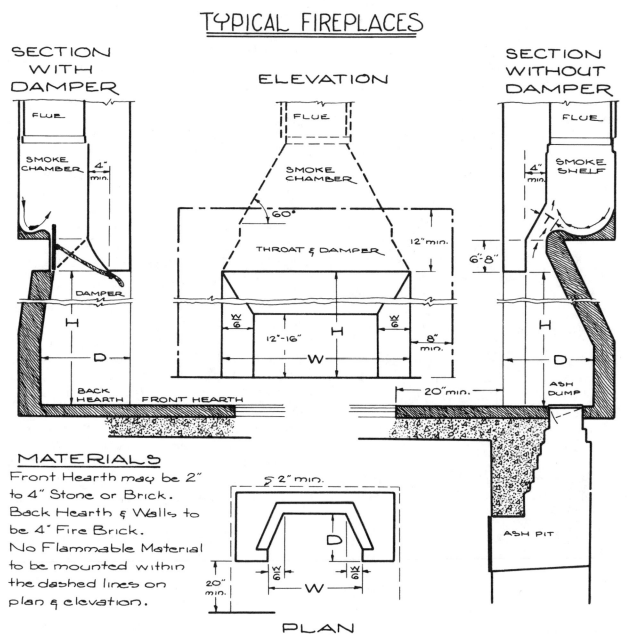

SECTION WITH DAMPER

FLUE

SMOKE CHAMBER

4" min.

DAMPER

H

D

BACK HEARTH

FRONT HEARTH

ELEVATION

FLUE

SMOKE CHAMBER

60°

THROAT & DAMPER

12" min.

W/6   W/6

12"-16"   H

W

8" min.

20" min.

SECTION WITHOUT DAMPER

FLUE

SMOKE SHELF

4" min.

6"-8"

H

D

ASH DUMP

ASH PIT

NOT TO SCALE

MATERIALS

Front Hearth may be 2" to 4" Stone or Brick. Back Hearth & Walls to be 4" Fire Brick. No Flammable Material to be mounted within the dashed lines on plan & elevation.

PLAN

2" min.

D

20" min.

W/6   W/6

W

FIREPLACE PROPORTION	
W	24 - 84
H	2/3 to 3/4 × W
D	1/2 to 2/3 × H
FLUE AREA	1/10 of W × H
T - AREA	5/4 to 3/2 FLUE AREA
T - WIDTH	3" min. - 4½" max.

Note : All Dimensions shown are in inches.

APPROPRIATE FLUE SIZES		
FIREPLACE WIDTH	RECTANGULAR INSIDE DIM.	ROUND IN. DIA.
24	7¼ × 7¼	8
30 - 34	7 × 11½	10
36 - 44	11¼ × 11¼	12
46 - 56	11¼ × 16¼	15
58 - 68	15¾ × 15¾	18
70 - 84	17 × 21	22

A living room ceiling in an adobe home is traditionally vigas and herringbone, although it may be any other type that you may prefer. Living room walls are susceptible to a host of treatments, from painted, unplastered adobe walls, wood paneling, half paneling, painting or even wallpaper. The floor can be brick, adobe, tile, wood of several types, or carpeting. Hand-made Spanish style tin fixtures help create an authentic traditional adobe style with heavy wood furniture of the Spanish or Mediterranean styling. Don't forget bookcases, either built into a thick wall, or free-standing. Shelves and cabinets may also be built-in, and can be decorative as well as useful. We could go on and on regarding trim, coping, etc., but these all become matters of personal taste, and must be resolved to suit you.

A separate dining room is now somewhat rare, as the trend is toward dining areas of a less formal nature, which may be only an ell or alcove off the living room or kitchen. However, if you want a formal dining room, it's your home, do what you please.

A utility room should be included in all homes without basements, which includes the majority of adobe homes. This room will contain the heating plant, hot water heater, and perhaps washer and dryer. It can also include shelving and storage, and perhaps even a small workshop. The utility room does not have to be a stark, drab room for function only, but can be brightly painted and decorated to the same basic scheme as the rest of the home at very little extra cost. If the washer and dryer, and ironing or mending facilities are located here, the woman of the house will spend a good deal of time in it, as you may also if you install a small workshop, so make it at least bearable, if not downright attractive.

Dens, studies, offices, family or play rooms may all be incorporated into the floor plan of your adobe home, again depending upon your own needs and desires. For a young, growing family, the floor plan can be laid out so that future room additions may be built without disrupting use of the initial construction. This requires that your planning will anticipate this future need, and perhaps even detailed plans will be made at once, so that the room to be added later will have direct access to the rest of the home, without impeding the use of other rooms.

CHAPTER XV

Portals, Patios And Landscaping

The portal, or porch, is an essential element of the true adobe home, whether Pueblo or Territorial styling, and is an important aesthetic feature, as well as protecting the home's entrance-way from the elements, and simply for a place to sit and enjoy a pleasant summer's eve.

A portal is not a gobbed-on excrescence, but an integral segment of the home. It may be relatively short, in filling the space between two wings of the home; or it can be quite long, perhaps running the full length of two walls. The portal is not built as an addition onto the house, but is rather planned, designed and constructed as part of the home, to blend it all into a harmonious whole.

The design and construction of a portal will differ only in trim and finish from Pueblo to Territorial styling, as the basic components of foundation, floor, columns, caps or corbels, lintels, vigas and roof all must meet the same criteria of location and strength, whatever the styling. As with the rest of the house, a portal is designed and built from below the ground upward. The foundation of the portal is tied into the home foundation, and may be an extension or wing of the concrete foundation wall. The thickness of the portal's foundation will depend upon the weight of the portal, and thus its styling. Most portals are completely open from the floor to the roof, but there are some styles that include a waist-high wall or rail around the portal's outer edge. If Territorial styling,

this railing will be wood, and will not greatly influence the foundation loading. However, if a Pueblo-style rail or wall is built, the foundation wall must be thicker than the adobe block portal wall. A spread footing below the foundation wall will probably be required, again depending on the underlying soils.

The floor support of the portal may be any of the methods discussed for the home, although most are now concrete slabs on grade. The floor surfacing of the portal may be anything that you wish, from the bare concrete of the slab, wood, brick, tile, or even brick or stone veneers. Each of the portal's columns will be erected upon a short pedestal base, and both pedestal and column are secured to the portal floor with through-bolts. The columns will be at least six inches thick, generally round for Pueblo and square for Territorial styles. The spacing of the columns will accord with the size of the lintel beam, and the weight of the roof, varying from six to twelve or more feet apart.

Each column will be topped with a cap, to transfer the loading from the lintel to the column. The caps are most often square in cross-section, with a trapezoidal shape. The accompanying illustration shows several variations of lintels, columns and caps, and their decorative possibilities. The pattern selected for the caps and columns may be very effective, if carried throughout various wood trim, window and door lintels, and even the interior of the home. The lintel

TYPICAL LINTELS, CAPS & COLUMNS
May be Constructed from 2 x 6 or 6 x 6
Lumber - Natural, Stained or Painted Finish

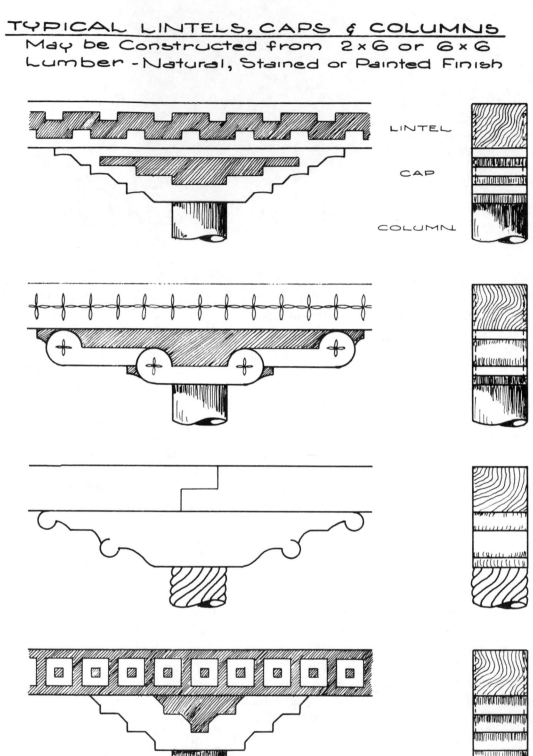

LINTEL

CAP

COLUMN

SIDE VIEWS   END

LINTELS ARE MOST OFTEN SQUARE, SELDOM ROUND.
CAPS ARE SQUARE CROSS-SECTION, BOTH MAY USE AN
INCISED HAND-CARVED PATTERN. BRACKETS WILL BE
HALF-CAP SECTIONS. COLUMNS MAY BE ROUND OR
SQUARE, SOMETIMES FLUTED OR CARVED. CHOOSE ONE
GENERAL PATTERN, & WITH MINOR VARIATIONS, USE THROUGHOUT.

is at least a 6x6 beam, or may be made up of multiple 2x6s or larger. The lintel will run the entire perimeter of the portal to support the roof.

In some Pueblo-style variations, particularly with a waist-high adobe wall, the columns are made of reinforced adobe blocks, and the complete portal exterior is plastered. This gives a massive aspect to the portal, which must suit the design of the home. This treatment is most effective when the adobe columns are comparatively long, and the tops of adjoining columns are flared together to form an arch. However, this arch construction will be complex, whether you attempt to lay block arches, or even use concrete poured into heavy arch forms, then plaster the complete portal.

The portal roof and parapet can be any of the types for the home, although it will not need to be as substantial, and the insulation may be omitted, unless it is planned to enclose the portal with windows, as a sort of winter porch. Vigas on Pueblo styles will project beyond the lintel, whereas the vigas on Territorial homes frequently are boxed in. The parapet on the portal will have the same treatment as the main roof parapet, that is, rounded adobe for Pueblo, and brick coping for Territorial.

The complete exterior of the home will blend into the same trim and styling as the portal, so that window and door frames, lintels, and possibly shutters will be one basic, harmonious style. Don't attempt to introduce too many variations in trim or decoration either inside or outside the home, as one basic pattern will avoid clashing of styles, and afford more pleasing long-term aesthetic values. You may be living in this home for many years, so don't go very far out on fad trims or extreme styling, as moderation wears much better over the long haul.

The total aspect of the home-site deserves considerable attention in your planning, although you probably wish to save all the landscaping until the time after you have moved into the home. Many people will spend as much as several years after the home has been completed in finishing the outside planting, patios, walks,

walls, etc. But don't just ignore the landscaping until you are ready to do it, as it can affect the placement of the home on the site, and influence some of your decisions on layout and design. Give at least basic consideration to the site planning and landscaping during your initial planning, so that a concept of needs and locations will at least have been evolved.

Every adobe home demands a patio, whether for aesthetic effect, or the sheer joy of sitting out there on your duff on a pleasant day. The patio can be the hub of outside activities around the home and the focal point of much of the landscaping. Its size, shape and location are integrated with the design of the home and the total effect of home, patio and landscaping. It may lie enclosed within an ell of the home, fill an area in the back, or even ramble about at several levels. It may be almost any surface type from flagstone to brick, or bare concrete. The actual construction of a patio is, again, a whole lot of hard work, but will be well worth the effort expended. Depending upon the soil of your home-site, the base of the patio may be either several inches of sand or concrete. The flagstone, brick, tile, or whatever, are laid in mortar on top of the base, with each individual piece leveled, and joints filled with mortar. That sounds simple enough, but as with most simple explanations, it covers one helluva lot of work.

A patio does not have to be a plain, flat slab, as it can be laid at several levels, interspersed with raised flower beds, seats, tree planters, and perhaps a fountain and/or a fireplace. It may be contained within an adobe wall on all or several sides, and walks of the same material as the patio may spread from it throughout the property. The inherent decorative possibilities of patio and landscaping are limited only by your own ingenuity, time, and money. If you are like most of us, the patio and landscaping will become a long-term project, that most probably will not even be started until you have finished your adobe home.

Your landscaping should be laid out on a detailed scaled plot at the same time as initial planning for the home is undertaken, even though no work may be done on the landscaping until the home is completed. This detail plot is required at the first stages to both properly locate the home on the site, and to evaluate the best use or change in the ground surface of the site. If you took the soil for the adobe brick from the homesite, there is a large hole or depression to be either filled, or extended, so that the spot may have further use. Consider how the land should slope away from the home, both for drainage protection and aesthetics. The home is either located on the high point of the site, or it must be protected from runoff and surface drainage. This could require cutting away some portions of the soil to give slopes away from the house.

Landscaping for the adobe home should be in character with the home itself, and serves to set off the lines of the home. The adobe home is best suited to informal landscaping of Southwestern character, which can be quite effectively done even on small lots. Adobe or rock walls are a traditional and excellent element of such landscaping, and give opportunity for considerable variety. Rock gardens, cactus, pinon, juniper, and other arid country shrubs and trees, lend themselves to low-maintenance and hardy life. The property may be roughly divided into public, private and service areas, each of which can be quite different. The public area is generally the front of the house, or the facade that is visible from the street, road or driveway. The landscaping of this area is not showy, but informal placement of trees, shrubs or small flower beds to set off the lines of the home. One of the traditional characteristics of the adobe home is that this so-called public area is frequently completely eliminated by surrounding the street or road side of the home with a line of trees, tall shrubs, or a high adobe wall.

The service area is just that, an area set aside for clothes lines, garbage cans, wood storage for the fireplaces, and other such items. This area is usually on the border of the home-site, perhaps on an alley, and can be screened from the landscaped areas with a wall, fence, trees or shrubs. The private area will be that portion of the site which is used for the play, hobbies, cut flower gardens, patio and the general pleasure of the family. This area will be landscaped only to please the family or guests, and may be done any way you darn well care to do it.

You will probably have a one or two car garage, either attached to the house, or as a separate building, perhaps including a workshop. A garage can be built to the same basic style as the home, and from the same materials. There is a growing tendency to insulate the complete structure of garages, both from their use as work areas, and due to the possibility of their conversion to living space for expanding families. The location and material of the driveway depend upon the location of the home-site, the garage's location on that site, and the general size and use of the site, plus the direction and distance of the connecting street or road. On many small urban lots, there is not much choice, as the garage is usually attached at one side of the home, and the driveway must proceed directly from it to the street. Rock or adobe walls can be used to edge these short drives, and isolate them from other use areas, as may shrubs or trees. For the larger site, a curved or half-moon drive may be desirable, with two entrances. Urban driveways, particularly short ones, are most often concrete, although asphalt and gravel run close behind. The usually longer rural drive is generally gravel or asphalt, as that quantity of concrete will get into a good bit of expense, whether it's ready-mix or roll-your own, and also a lot of work.

If you have a large enough site and wallet, you may wish to build a one-room guest house to accommodate either the mother-in-law, or paying guests, that is, rentals. These small guest houses are very prevalent in the Southwest, and can be adaptable to offices, studios, study, den, or simple hiding place. The design, construction, decoration and trim can be the same as the main home, although one that is isolated or screened from the home can be any contrast you might wish.

You might have hoped that we would include data on flowers, shrubs or trees, and the proper

ADOBE GUEST HOUSE

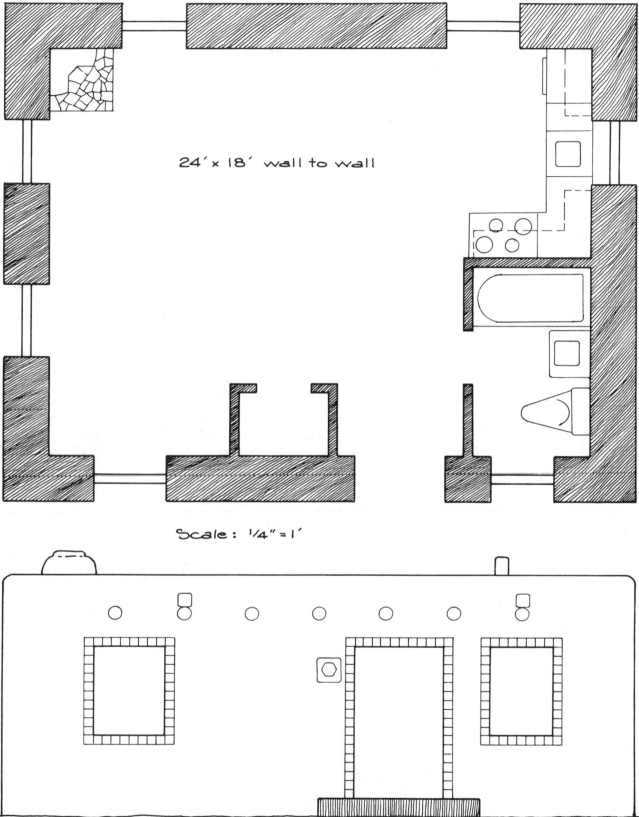

24' x 18' wall to wall

Scale: 1/4" = 1'

care and feeding thereof. We had considered doing this; however, as an adequately stabilized adobe block home can now be built almost anywhere, we decided not to include any such listings. There is too much variety in soil and climatic conditions to assert that only such-and-such or so-and-so may be used around adobe homes. Anyway, there are already so darn many books that involve nothing but landscaping and gardening, that we felt we could get in over our heads, as we definitely have a black, rather than green, thumb.

At any rate, we hope that we have either stimulated your thoughts, or solidified plans, so that you will indeed build your own adobe dream home. The entire project may take years to complete, and buckets of sweat, but it will be worth it, if you carry out your dream.

CHAPTER XVI

Photographic Details

PUEBLO

FACADES

ON

PUBLIC

BUILDINGS

PUEBLO
DETAILS

TERRITORIAL
DETAILS

ADOBE
DETAILS

ADOBE
DETAILS

SPOOL
&
TERRITORIAL
WINDOWS

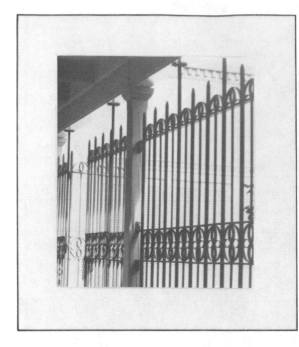

ORNAMENTAL IRONWORK

ADOBE
WALLS

ADOBE
WALLS

PUEBLO
ENTRIES

HERRINGBONE
CEILINGS

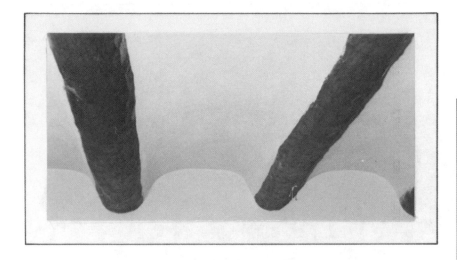

OTHER
ADOBE
CEILING
STYLES

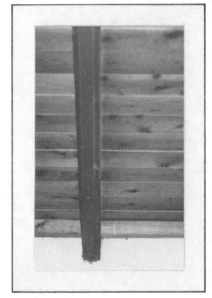

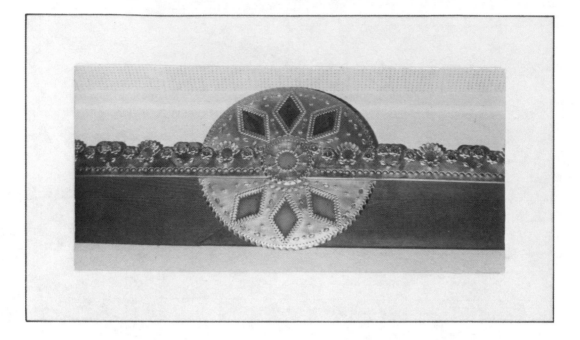

DECORATIVE TINWORK

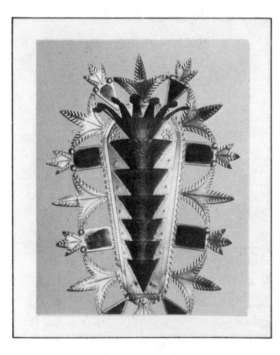

INTERIOR
IRONWORK

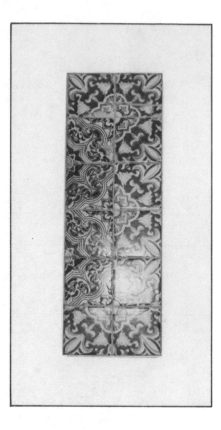

MEXICAN
TILE

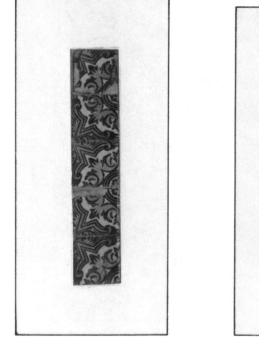

ADOBE
FIREPLACES

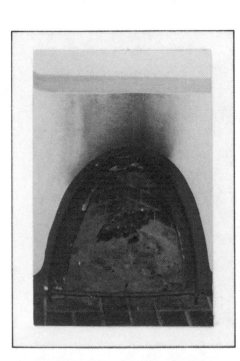

ADOBE
FIREPLACES

INTERIOR
DETAILS

ONE STARTED -

ANOTHER COMPLETED